Conservatories

A COMPLETE GUIDE

Planning, Managing and Completing Your Conservatory

Conservatories

A COMPLETE GUIDE

Planning, Managing and Completing Your Conservatory

Julian Owen

THE CROWOOD PRESS

First published in 2005 by
The Crowood Press Ltd
Ramsbury, Marlborough
Wiltshire SN8 2HR

www.crowood.com

British Library Cataloguing-in-Publication Data
A catalogue record for this book is available from the British Library.

ISBN 1 86126 726 6

Disclaimer
The author and publisher do not accept any responsibility, in any manner whatsoever for any error, or omission, nor any loss, damage, injury, adverse outcome or liability of any kind incurred as a result of the use of any of the information contained in this book, or reliance upon it.

Designed and edited by Focus Publishing, 11a St Botolph's Road, Sevenoaks, Kent TN13 3AJ

Printed and bound in Malaysia by Times Offset (M) Sdn Bhd

Contents

ABOUT THE AUTHOR

Julian Owen MBE RIBA FRSA is a chartered architect who has been helping people build and improve their homes for many years. He has written books, magazine articles, judged competitions and presented seminars on the subject of improving, designing and constructing homes. He runs his own practice in the East Midlands, carrying out a wide variety of domestic and commercial projects. In 1993 he and a colleague founded ASBA, the architects' network specializing in domestic projects. The network membership is made up of locally based architects across the UK. Julian Owen was awarded an MBE for services to architecture in 2003.

DEDICATION

For Chris Salisbury, my father-in-law, friend and the best granpa a family could ever have wished for.

ACKNOWLEDGEMENTS

Most of the companies and organizations whose assistance I have gratefully received whilst writing this book are listed under Useful Contacts, but I would particularly like to mention Conservatories Online, an excellent website that has provided invaluable information, and Brian Garner of Town and Country Conservatories who has assisted me with the benefit of his many years' experience working as a conservatory designer.

I am indebted to Zoe Cockcroft, who, with her usual dedication and thoroughness, has helped me to sort out much of the paperwork and correspondence, and to my father, Richard Owen, who has patiently checked the manuscript, offering tactful, constructive criticism. I would also like to thank my wife, Jill, and daughters Katy and Sophie, for all their love and support during the writing of this book.

(Town & Country Masterworks in Glass)

(Amdega Ltd)

(Lisa Moth for Vale Garden Houses Ltd)

(Holloways Conservatory Furniture & Garden Ornament.
Photographer: Bob Challenor)

FIGS 1–4 *There are many different designs for conservatories.*

CHAPTER 1

Introduction

Most of us have a keen interest in our homes and are constantly searching for ways to improve them. Modern living seems to require more and more gadgets, and the availability of cheap furniture means that we always need just a little bit more space than we actually have. We like to be seen as people with taste and an eye for style and we expect the best products to be available to us. These may seem to be modern pre-occupations, but they have actually been with us for a long time. It is for these reasons that conservatories first became a desirable addition to the average house and continue to be the most popular home improvement choice. Over £1 billion was spent in the UK on conservatories in 2002 and this amount has continued to grow at an accelerated rate.

There is a huge industry that has grown up to design, manufacture and construct conservatories for homeowners. The wide choice offers a wonderful range of options but plenty of pitfalls for the unwary. How do you decide whether or not a conservatory is right for your house? Should you believe the salesman who paints a glowing picture of domestic bliss if you buy from him or her? How do you ensure that you get the best possible design for your money? What can you do to find responsible suppliers and avoid the dreaded 'cowboy builders'? This book will answer all of these questions and many more, and will help to make the task of acquiring a new, special room for your house an enjoyable venture.

A SHORT HISTORY OF CONSERVATORIES

The modern conservatory has a long ancestry that can be traced from the ancient world through to the Renaissance and later the Victorians, right up to the familiar modern version. The stylish glass buildings that we add on to our homes today have their origins in far more spectacular structures that were once only available to the privileged few. The story could be started with the Romans, if you allow for the fact that they had to use sheets of mica, a kind of transparent rock, rather than glass. In Renaissance times, temporary timber sheds were built around delicate plants to protect them each winter. The development of the modern concept of a conservatory began properly in the eighteenth century, unexpectedly owing much to a humble citrus fruit. As countries such as Britain and France began to expand into the world and develop their empires, new countries were discovered, overflowing with unknown and exciting species of plants. Many cuttings and specimens were shipped

---

Myths About Conservatories

- They are a cheap way of extending your house.
- They are an investment that you will always get back when you sell your house.
- You never need Planning Permission to build one.
- It will be too expensive to get an architect to help.
- You have to go to a specialist supplier to get one.
- They are unusable in summer and too cold in winter.
- They should be on the south-facing side of a house.

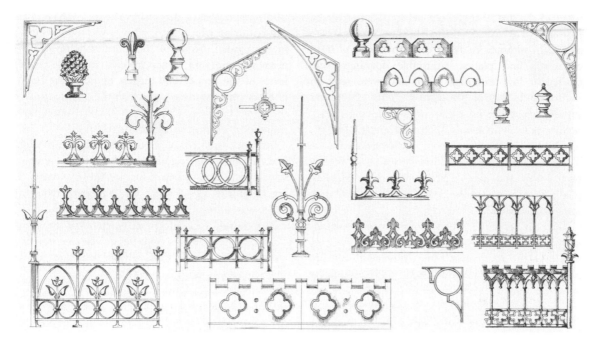

FIG. 5 (OPPOSITE) Glass houses were a popular feature on large houses and mansions. (Oak Leaf Conservatories Ltd)

FIG. 6 The Victorians created a range of standard features for their conservatories. (Lisa Moth for Vale Garden Houses Ltd)

home, only to perish in a climate that was alien to them. The Western European winter was particularly lethal to plants used to a hot climate.

Orange trees were particularly fashionable, thanks to Louis XIV and his extravagant gardens at Versailles, which featured them extensively. The problem of keeping them alive was solved by putting them in large tubs and moving them indoors into 'orangeries'. These buildings began as simple wooden sheds, which had many windows but only a normal tiled roof. As glass manufacturing techniques improved, glass became available in sheets that were stronger, thinner and cheaper, so the windows became larger and the roofs were glazed. A further innovation was the introduction of heating systems, designed to control temperature and humidity.

By the early 1800s, a revolution in the design and construction of glasshouses was taking place. Techniques of manufacturing cast iron had been mastered, producing components ideally suited to supporting the ever-larger sheets of glass. This high technology lent itself to prefabrication and Victorian

architects were quick to realize the potential for creating large, elegant structures, formed from what seemed to be an impossibly thin cast-iron framework. All of this ingenuity culminated in the Crystal Palace, built in London in 1851. It caused a sensation and the opportunity to exploit the popularity of this new kind of building was not missed by entrepreneurs, who began to make scaled-down versions that could be added to even the more humble of middle-class homes.

Up until this point, conservatories and green-houses had generally been found in stately homes and mansions. The owners of these properties displayed their wealth and power by growing exotic plants in defiance of the natural climate. Now this privilege became more widely available. Improvements in methods of storage and transportation brought down the cost of importing plants. So as well as being able to add an extension built from the latest 'high-tech' material, Victorian homeowners could buy plenty of unusual ferns, shrubs and flowers to fill it with.

Glass is not a good insulator, however, so in order

11

CHAPTER 2

The Benefits of a Conservatory

DO YOU REALLY NEED A CONSERVATORY?

Adding a conservatory has the potential to transform the whole of the ground floor of a house. It can improve the way that rooms are used and circulated through and add a new, exciting space for families to enjoy. But before you are caught up in the thrill of choosing a design and getting it built, it is worth taking a step back and making sure that a conservatory is really what you need. Once you realize the ways that a conservatory can improve both the look of your home and your lifestyle, and have called in a salesman, it may be too late to make a detached decision. Think through all the options before you get too far into the process. Conservatories can bring many benefits if they are added in the right way to an appropriate property, but they can also end up creating unloved, little-used spaces that fail to live up to the early dream. The way to avoid yours befalling this fate is to be sure that your particular requirements will be satisfied, confirm that there is an appropriate place to fit one on to the house, and then make sure that it is carefully designed in a way that suits your needs.

Start by writing a list of the reasons that you think a conservatory will be a worthwhile investment. Do this in conjunction with the rest of your family, or anyone else who lives with you and will be affected by the change. For example, you may just need extra room or you may be a keen gardener with a need for somewhere to grow new types of plants that would not otherwise survive the British climate. Then look at the list with a critical eye. Is there an alternative

solution that will do the same things, only better or cheaper? If you are unsure, it is well worth talking to an independent professional such as an architect or landscape designer as well as the conservatory designer or supplier. Remember that everyone has a vested interest – the sales representative wants to earn a commission and the architect will be hoping to be asked to design a new extension. In the end, you have to make up your own mind – do not be persuaded to launch into anything if you have any significant doubts. You are the expert on your own requirements, and anyone else can only advise.

They are many reasons why you may eventually plump for a conservatory as the answer to your prayers, and it is worth considering each aspect in relation to your project.

Additional Space

The single most likely reason for acquiring a conservatory is to make your house bigger. It is an easy way to create another room, or extend an existing one. It is not difficult to visualize how your house might look and feel once one has been built, and conservatories are an ever-popular solution to an overcrowded house. Sometimes there is a need for a complete new room, perhaps because the family is growing and developing. Many houses have been built to very tight space requirements, with the standard arrangement of kitchen, living room and dining room. There may be a need for a room for family activities, or even just somewhere to help accommodate the furniture

FIG. 9 (OPPOSITE) A conservatory can add a large amount of extra space to your home. (Amdega Ltd)

and possessions most people acquire. Conservatories provide fun, flexible, informal spaces that can be used for sitting quietly while enjoying the garden on a summer's evening, for dinner parties, or by the kids for doing their homework. During the day they have the added benefit of appearing to be bigger than they really are. A relatively small conservatory will feel much bigger than the same floor area enclosed by four walls.

Design

There is a wide range of design options, with all kinds of layouts, styles and materials to choose from. Period styles such as ornate Victorian and more sober Georgian are readily available, along with modern and high tech designs for a more contemporary look. The relatively 'lightweight' construction contrasts with the solid masonry of the main house, and can allow a change of style without spoiling the overall appearance of a property as long as it is sensitively designed. An appropriate design will improve the appearance of a house, and add a sense of quality that the original house may be lacking. Because the designs are based on standard components it is relatively easy to be actively involved in the design process or choose a design from a supplier's pattern book.

Well-Being

Most people retain a powerful image of the feeling of well-being that a good conservatory can create, and associate this with sunlight, fresh air and a pleasant atmosphere. Consequently, conservatories can offer a relaxing 'chill-out zone' quite different in character to the rest of the house, that could not be easily achieved by other means. It will prolong the time that can be spent in close proximity to the outdoors – when it is too cold to sit out in winter, the conservatory will still be a warm place to sit and enjoy the garden. There is an affliction called Seasonally Affected Disorder (or SADS), in which sufferers experience depression as a result of the shorter daylight hours in the winter. Some sufferers can be

FIG. 10 (OPPOSITE) Extraordinary and unexpected buildings can be created using glass. (Oak Leaf Conservatories Ltd)

FIG. 11 Glass can be used to create modern designs. (Apropos Clear Span. Photographer: James White)

helped by exposure to increased daylight levels, and most people benefit psychologically from an increased exposure to daylight and the sun.

Daylight

An ordinary extension to a house will join on to an existing room or rooms of a house, making it deeper, and the light from any windows will have to penetrate further into the building. This means that unless windows can be introduced into the wall on the side of the house (which is usually facing the boundary), the back of the room will become more gloomy, and therefore less pleasant during daylight hours. In contrast to this, the glazed walls of a conservatory allow the maximum light possible into the

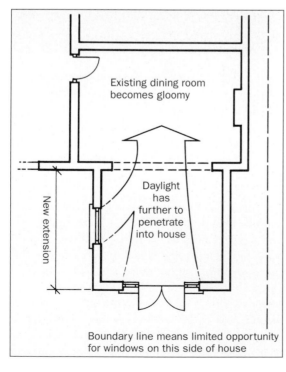

Existing dining room becomes gloomy

New extension

Daylight has further to penetrate into house

Boundary line means limited opportunity for windows on this side of house

FIG. 12 (ABOVE LEFT) *A good place to 'chill out'. (Lisa Moth for Vale Garden Houses Ltd)*

FIG. 13 (ABOVE RIGHT) *Glass will let daylight into the existing house. (Apropos Clear Span. Photographer: Hugh Palmer)*

FIG. 14 *A normal extension may reduce the daylight reaching inside the house.*

house, and cause only a slight reduction in daylight. In fact, if an existing window is replaced by glazed doors or an opening, the net effect will be an increase in the natural lighting level. This factor will often tilt the balance when trying to decide between a solid brick or a glazed extension.

Sunlight

Conservatories have a mixed benefit with relation to the sun. A badly sited extension will overheat and become unusable. 'Badly sited' often means facing due south, which sometimes comes as a surprise to potential purchasers but not to anyone who has owned a conservatory with this orientation. A correctly sited conservatory, perhaps used in conjunction with solid masonry walls, can make the best use of the natural energy produced by the sun to keep the space warmer in spring and autumn and extend the amount of time that it remains comfortable without heating. The 'greenhouse effect', which traps in heat and is responsible for the unwanted heat build-up in summer is a positive benefit at these times. This effect is prolonged where the solid masonry walls of the house soak up heat during the day and radiate it back into the conservatory after dusk.

Relationship with Garden

A reason why many gardeners find conservatories an essential addition to their home is that the concentration of the sun's rays combined with a carefully controlled heating system extends the range of plants that can be grown to include species that would not survive the outside climate, but need more sunlight than would be available in a normal room. With a

FIG. 15 More sunlight can be a benefit to a room. (Town & Country Masterworks in Glass)

large garden, the conservatory can provide an attractive transition space between the inside and outside of the house. If the garden is very small a conservatory is less likely to dominate the space than other kinds of extension, and will not overshadow or shade any plants that are growing outside.

SPEED

There are a number of reasons why adding a conservatory is a relatively quick process. If it is provided by a company that designs and constructs conservatories as a single service, this reduces the time wasted waiting for a contractor to become available after the design work has been completed, because the job has been programmed in as soon as an instruction was given to proceed. Another cause of delay can be waiting for the local authority to grant Planning and Building Regulations approval. Often neither of these is required, or, in the case of Building Regulations, can be dealt with fairly quickly because the construction is standardized and can be approved without detailed drawings.

FIG. 16 A conservatory is a good way of bringing the garden into the house.

FIG. 17 A simple
conservatory is quick
to build.

DIY CONSTRUCTION

Because many conservatories are produced as a kit of parts, prefabricated to a high degree of precision, they lend themselves to DIY construction. Although the foundations, floor and dwarf walls are usually conventionally built, above these the construction is mainly an exercise in assembly, within the range of skills of an enthusiastic amateur. There are kits and even special foundation and wall systems designed to make construction easier. Many builders' merchants and specialist suppliers will provide a design and delivery service, leaving the rest up to you. A conservatory is an easier DIY project to take on than an extension with a tiled roof. There are fewer building skills that have to be mastered and the project is quicker to complete.

ADDING VALUE

Generally speaking, a conservatory will increase the value of your home, but not by the amount that it has cost you to build it. In a typical situation, adding a conservatory or other kind of extension may only add about half the build cost to the value of the property. This means that there is a price that you are paying that you are unlikely to recover when you sell the house. So if you expect to move in the next few years after the conservatory has been built you should question carefully whether you should be doing it at all. However, you may still decide to go ahead in order to increase the quality of your life, something very difficult to measure in monetary terms.

One way to look at it is to assess the benefits to your lifestyle that the new space will add, estimate

21

FIG. 18 An extension has to be mostly glass to be defined as a conservatory under the Building Regulations. (Rutland County Ltd)

how long you are likely to live in the house, and calculate the actual cost of acquiring the conservatory. This can then be fed into a simple calculation that will tell you how much you are paying each year for the benefit of having the conservatory: take the cost of conservatory plus the new house value minus the original house value divided by the number of years the house is to be lived in. For example:

Cost of conservatory	= £10,000
New value of house	= £106,000
Original house value	= £100,000
Actual cost of conservatory	
= £10,000 − (£106,000 − £100,000)	
	= £4,000
Number of years in the house	= five
£4,000 divided by five	= £800.

This, plus heating and maintenance costs, is how much you are paying for the use of the conservatory. If you do not intend to move for ten years, it drops to £400. These approximate figures can be compared

with moving costs, which include solicitor's and agent's fee, removal costs, stamp duty, and so on. In the example above these could be more than the actual conservatory cost.

This type of analysis emphasizes the importance of making the right decision to proceed, and then ensure that you get the best possible end result.

ALTERNATIVES TO A CONSERVATORY

There are several alternatives to adding a conservatory, and these should be considered before making a financial commitment. For example, a halfway-house between a conservatory and a conventional extension is a sun room, in which the walls are glazed but the roof is solid and insulated, possibly with some rooflights to help daylight levels.

Unfortunately there does not seem to be any fixed definitions for conservatories and conservatory-like buildings and rooms. Different countries and even suppliers within the countries all use the descriptions to mean different things. However, there are some basic building types that use glass to form a significant part of their construction, and the following descriptions cover the main ones.

Single-Glazed-Wall Conservatory

Most people know a conservatory when they see one, but sometimes not all the walls are glazed. Occasionally one is built with only a single glazed wall and a glazed roof. The Building Regulations contain the closest thing to an official description of what makes a room a conservatory. They state that if it has 75 per cent of its ceiling area and 50 per cent of its wall area made up of a clear or translucent material, it is deemed to be a conservatory for the purposes of the Regulations.

Greenhouse

Obviously, a greenhouse is a conservatory with plants in. But to properly qualify it should not be used by people to sit in as part of the house and should not be heated.

Sun Room

For some people, this is just another name for a conservatory. But it is a good description for rooms that have fully glazed walls down to at least sill level, plus a solid roof with rooflights. The resulting space has some of the benefits of a conservatory, in that there is plenty of light and potential for sunlight. However, in summer when there is a hot sun overhead, the insulated roof and blinds on the rooflights do a reasonable job in keeping the internal temperature down. In winter it can be heated economically.

Orangery

A description with historic connotations, this typically is used to describe a room that has walls made up of vertical strips of glazing interspersed with masonry. There is usually more of the glass than there is of the stone or brick. Parapets conceal gutters behind a decorated frieze and the roof is entirely of glass, sometime with a decorative lantern. The term is often used rather loosely to describe a single-storey room that has normal walls for a house but an entirely glazed roof.

FIG. 19 When does a conservatory become a greenhouse? (Amdega Ltd)

Comparison of a Conservatory with an Extension and a Sun Room			
Feature	Conservatory	Extension	Sun Room (Solid Roof)
Cost	Less good	Good	Average
Daylight in the rest of the house	Very good	Less good	Average
South-facing wall	Less good	Good	Good
Extra space	Good	Good	Good
Performance in winter	Poor	Very good	Average
Self-build	Good	Less good	Less good
Relationship with garden	Very good	Less good	Average
Two storeys of space	Less good	Very good	Less good
Versatility of use	Average	Less good	Good
Resale after short period	Less good	Less good	Less good
Well-being	Very good	Less good	Average
Design possibilities	Good	Good	Less good
Ease of procurement	Very good	Less good	Less good
Speed of design/construction	Very good	Less good	Less good
Noise in the rain	Less good	Good	Average

MAKING THE DECISION

Before you make the decision to build, you should also consider the option of moving house altogether, along with the other choices that are available to you.

Adding a conservatory may not be ideal if:
- You are likely to move in the near future anyway.
- The garden is relatively small.
- The conservatory required would be very large in comparison to the house.

You should build a conventional extension or sun room if:
- You need a space that is easy to make comfortable all year round and don't want higher heating costs.
- The wall side of the house that will be extended faces due south and you want to use the space all of the summer.
- You wish to use the space in the winter, but minimize heating costs.
- You want the cheapest extra space possible.

Don't add any kind of extension if:
- You can replan the existing house to create more space (for example, convert a garage).
- You will need to add the cost on to an already high mortgage.
- A cheaper greenhouse will do the same job for plant propagation.

CHAPTER 3

Conservatory Design

One of the hardest steps in the process of acquiring a conservatory is moving on from the fantasy fuelled by pictures of glamorous houses in the magazines and sales brochures, to the reality of getting one designed for your own property. If you approach this process step by step and do your homework before you finally place your order, you will increase the chances of a well-designed and appropriate additional room for your home.

Among the things that you must assess early in the design process are how much you can afford and how long you can expect the various stages to take. Both vary enormously between different projects and it is important to decide on these early on and set some targets.

DRAWING UP A BUDGET

Obtaining finance for alterations and extensions is easier for private householders now than it has ever been. Building societies and other lenders will usually be happy to lend the money for a project provided that the equity in the house will cover it and you are earning enough to cover the repayments. But you should not set your budget based on the maximum finance that you have available. A glance at the section in Chapter 2 on 'Adding Value' will tell you that you should think carefully about how long you are going to live in the house, as well as how big the conservatory really needs to be.

You also have to decide whether you will go for the biggest, cheapest conservatory, or a smaller, higher quality design. As a general rule, unless your budgetary constraints are very tight, it is not a good idea to

go for the cheapest available system. A cheap, poorly built, badly designed structure can actually reduce the value of your home, will cost more in maintenance in the long run and may be unusable for longer periods as a result of weather conditions. On the other hand, it is easier to spend more money than it is to stick to a budget and the better quality conservatories are an expensive luxury item. To help make your decision on the quality you should go for, try to be objective about your house and match it in quality to an equivalent in the wide range of conservatories available. So, a large five bedroom listed town house can comfortably take a well-made hardwood conservatory without it looking out of place, whereas a conservatory of similar quality may not look right on the average suburban semi-detached house. In the latter case, there is also far less chance of covering some of your outlay as value added to the sale price when you move on.

At 2004 prices, the cost of an average kit conservatory is about £12,000 to £14,000, but you can spend a lot more, for example £30,000 on a 16sq m good quality bespoke design, including the building work. Larger conservatories can easily cost from £50,000 upwards. However, modern manufacturing methods mean that budget versions are cheaper than ever and you can purchase a kit from a DIY shop for as little as £4,000–£6,000, although the building work will be extra on top of this. You will not necessarily get this money back when you sell your house, but if it has been carefully chosen and integrates well with the house, you can expect to recover 50 to 70 per cent when you move.

Once you have set your budget, the most likely

Conservatory Budget

Item	Your Estimated Cost in £
Conservatory supply	
Conservatory fitting	
Building work – foundation, floor, dwarf walls, etc.	
Alterations and making good to the house	
Insurance costs	
Planning Application fees (if required)	
Building Regulations fee (if required)	
Blinds, louvres and shutters	
Finishes paint, floor tiles, etc.	
Plumbing	
Lighting and electrical work	
Mechanical ventilation and heating (if required)	
Extension of the security alarm	
Alterations and making good to the garden	
Making good to neighbour's garden or fence (if on the boundary)	
New furniture	

FIG. 22 A cheap and badly built conservatory will not enhance your home.

cause of any over-spending will be your failure to have recognized all of the costs that will be incurred. It is a good idea to start with a list of everything that you think will need to be done and to check it regularly, to remind yourself of where the money will be going. The chart on page 27 shows what some of these costs are likely to be. Of course, at the start you will not be able to fill in the amounts with any degree of accuracy, but as your project proceeds you will be able to pick off each one and either delete it as not applicable or put a real figure in as you get quotes or identify actual items that you are going to buy. You should certainly have completed this exercise with a reasonable degree of accuracy before you sign the order for the conservatory to be delivered.

HOW LONG WILL IT TAKE?

Given that adding a conservatory to your house is an important step, with significant implications for your lifestyle and finances, it is not something to rush into. It can take six or seven months from the point of ordering to moving in, particularly if Planning Permission has to be obtained before the work can start. You should allow a realistic period of time to get everything done. But if you are just starting to consider the idea, it is worth taking a little time to do your research before you launch into talking to sales representatives or designers. This alone could take a couple of months if you are diligent and only have weekends available for visits. You then have to draw up a shortlist of suppliers or designers, interview them and decide which to use.

The design process itself is likely to be fairly short unless it is integrated into other remodelling work planned for the house at the same time. You may or may not need to apply for Planning Permission, which takes at least eight weeks from the day the application is submitted to the day you get the permission notice in your hand. For all sorts of reasons explained later, if obtaining permission is necessary you must not allow work to start until it has been obtained. Assuming that the job is being well-managed, work will start shortly after this and can typically take anything from one to three months. Once the project has been finished and you

Acquiring a Conservatory – Timescale

Every project will be different, but these are some typical times that each stage may take.

Research Stage	Approach Designers and Suppliers	Design	Planning and Building Regulations (If required)	Pre-Contract	Construction	Post-Completion
1–3 months	1 month	2–4 weeks	8–10 weeks	1 week	3–10 weeks	3 months
Obtain magazines and brochures.	Compile shortlist of suppliers and designers.	Agree brief and budget with designer.	Wait 8 weeks for Planning Permission prior to commencing.	Inform insurers that work is about to start.	Construction of foundations and dwarf walls.	3 month period for defects to become apparent (if any).
Calculate budget.	Meet sales representatives.	Get existing house measured.	Obtain 'Full Plans Approval' or serve a Notice under the Building Regulations.	Meet contractors to agree working methods.	Conservatory fitted.	
Consult building society.	View previous work and talk to previous customers.	Approve draft sketches.		Inform neighbours.	Junctions with and work to existing house completed.	
Draw up a brief.		Agree price, start and completion dates.				
Visit DIY stores and conservatory showrooms.					Electrics, plumbing and fittings completed.	
Talk to people who have already done it.					Loose furniture and blinds fitted.	

A Typical 'To Do' List for a Conservatory Project

Item	Target Date	Actual Date
Obtain magazines and brochures		
Calculate budget		
Consult building society/bank		
Draw up brief		
Visit DIY stores and conservatory showrooms		
Talk to people who have already added a conservatory		
Compile shortlist of suppliers and designers		
Meet sales representatives		
View previous work and talk to customers		
Agree brief and budget with designer		
Get existing house measured		
Approve draft sketches		
Agree design, price, start and completion dates		
Apply for Planning Permission (if required)		
Apply for Building Control Approval (if required)		
Receive Planning Permission		
Receive Building Control Approval		
Start Party Wall process (if required)		
Order conservatory and building work		
Inform insurers that work is about to start		
Inform neighbours that work is about to start		
Meet contractors on site to agree working methods		
Construction of foundations and walls		
Conservatory delivered		
Conservatory erected		
Junctions with and work to existing house complete		
Electrical work complete		
Plumbing work complete		
Heating work complete		
Furniture and fittings installed		
Project complete		

occupy your conservatory, it is a good idea to agree with the builder that you will make an inspection three months later to check that no hidden defects have revealed themselves. There are some shortcuts that can be made, but unless you have an urgent need such as the imminent arrival of a baby or relative, it pays to appreciate that since you will be using the conservatory for many years to come, it is worth taking the time you need to ensure that you get the best possible result.

STARTING THE DESIGN PROCESS

One problem with conservatories is that they are sometimes more a testament to the skill of the salesmen than the requirements of their customers.

The bewildering range of options of style and materials, different types of plan and alternative ways of connecting to the house can be intimidating. However, a bit of time spent thinking and discussing the options as a family can help you to make the right choices. There are many house style magazines packed with good ideas, as well as plenty of well-illustrated free brochures available from suppliers and installers, all of which are good for providing inspiration and ideas for your own project. But before you begin to pick out which ones are most relevant and start to contact the professionals, you need to prepare an objective list of your requirements. This should be discussed and, hopefully, agreed with everyone in your family who is likely to use the new space. It should also be written down and kept as a record, to be checked regularly as the project progresses to

FIG. 23 A good-quality conservatory, however small, will enhance your home. (Rutland County Ltd)

ensure that you do not lose sight of your original aims. Designers call this list the project 'brief' and compiling one is an excellent way of focusing your mind on what you really need as opposed to what you would like (but probably can't afford).

FACTORS TO CONSIDER WHEN DESIGNING A CONSERVATORY

There are many aspects of design, some of which may not be relevant to your particular needs or situation. But it is worth considering as many of them as you can, however briefly; there may be a few surprises, since there are one or two common preconceptions that turn out not to be true.

Quality of Construction

One of the most crucial influences on the success of a design is the quality of the materials and construction that are to be used. Basic construction, with shallow, poorly built foundations, ill-designed details, inferior glazing type and cheap materials and construction will do more damage to the appearance and usability of the conservatory than any other design decision. Conversely, when these things are up to a good standard, even the smallest structure can be an attractive space to be in. A cheap conservatory, badly made and built, will not only be detrimental to your quality of life, but will also reduce the quality of your bank balance when the house is sold. In fact, as a general principle, it is better to spend a limited budget on the materials and construction rather than on frills and elaborations to the basic structure.

Style

The choice of the style of conservatory is a very personal one. One householder's beautifully elaborate design may appear gaudy and tacky to someone else. Likewise, what is seen to be a simple, elegantly proportioned structure by one proud owner, may just seem boring to another. While it is sensible to take the advice of the experts, beauty is in the eye of the beholder. You are paying and should stick out for what you want, although hopefully you will have done some research into the options before you reach to this point.

A major consideration is the design and style of the

Checklist

You should consider the following points when preparing a brief:

- How much can you afford for the whole project?
- How long do you expect to be in your house after the conservatory is finished?
- What is wrong with your house at the moment that you hope to solve by adding the conservatory?
- Who will use it?
- What will it be used for?
- Are you planning to use it for propagating plants as well as to live in?
- Will it be for guests, or just family and close friends?
- What furniture is intended to go into it (measure sizes for large items)?
- What time of year is it to be used?
- What time of day is it to be used?
- Should it be on just the ground floor, or could it go on the first floor or both floors?
- Where is there space around the house to add the conservatory?
- What rooms should it be connected to?
- Does it have to open out on to the garden?
- What are your preferences for the style?
- What construction and materials do you prefer?
- Will you need Planning Permission?
- Who will build it, that is, you, a builder, or a set of subcontractors employed by you?
- Will you need to buy new furniture for it?

---

house you are adding on to. A house built in the traditional style for the area in which you live, using local materials and basic construction detailing (known as the 'vernacular' style), will not usually be enhanced by the addition of a Victorian-style conservatory complete with octagonal plan and fancy decorative features. In these situations it is usually better to go for a simple, unadorned shape and use the best materials and construction that you can afford. In most cases, the roof should be made up of simple shapes, using a rectangular plan rather than a more elaborate design such as an octagon. This suggestion is even more applicable where the house is a genuine vernacular building rather than a modern imitation.

The spirit in which these types of houses were built was to use local materials such as stone, clay tiles and slate, which would have been easily available at the time, to the best effect. Adding one of the more elaborate styles on to such a building tends to leave the new addition looking like a modern afterthought, which, of course, is exactly what it is.

Period-style houses, built in one of the formal designs (as opposed to buildings created by traditional builders who just did what came naturally) can accommodate a wider range of styles, but it is a good idea to try to match the conservatory to the design of the house. However, if you are dealing with an older house, built when good-quality materials and craftsmanship were more readily available, it is better to go for a simple design in high-quality materials, such as hardwood, than add a lot of cheap imitation period details. Bespoke conservatories are more expensive but are able to adjust their proportions to suit the greater floor to ceiling height found in genuine

FIG. 24 (ABOVE) A simple design will look good against a house built to a traditional design. (Lisa Moth for Vale Garden Houses Ltd)

FIG. 25 A bespoke conservatory is essential to create a sensitive addition to a formal-style house. (Bartholomew Conservatories)

FIG. 26 (ABOVE) This design of conservatory would not fit comfortably up to the house, so a link has been used to join them together. (Bartholomew Conservatories. Designer: Dave Collings MBIAT)

FIG. 27 A similar technique has been used to join the conservatory to this house. (Bartholomew Conservatories)

FIG. 28 *The plan and proportions of these additions cleverly mimic the existing house. (Lisa Moth for Vale Garden Houses Ltd)*

FIG. 29 (OPPOSITE) *A classical design. (Glass Houses Ltd. Photographer: Hugh Palmer)*

Georgian, Victorian and Edwardian homes. Some of the 'off the peg' kit designs, developed to fit on to the back of the rather more squat housing found on modern estates, may look out of scale. Period houses also tend to be symmetrical in design and this should be respected in the layout of the conservatory.

If there are serious doubts about a conservatory blending in with the style of a house, particularly if the house has a large garden and imposing scale, it may be better to detach the conservatory from the house, either as a free-standing building, or with a visual break such as a glazed corridor as a link.

The style of conservatory is not decided just by the decoration and materials alone. It is also determined by the form of the plan, the proportions of the elevations and the way that the glass is divided up into panes.

When it comes to describing the various styles on offer, one problem is that the names tend to be picked by the marketing departments of the suppliers rather than complying with a set of standard rules. Historical accuracy has long been a casualty of their campaign to make the names of their products sound as attractive as possible and often the names have only the most tenuous of links to genuine architectural styles. The designers and suppliers do not seem to have reached a consensus, although there are some broad definitions that most will agree upon. The following is only an attempt to categorize the options available, but there is no point talking to a supplier about the style without seeing some pictures of what they actually look like.

Classical

Chunky, full-length columns, with decorated capitals (or tops), planned in rectangular shapes and gables

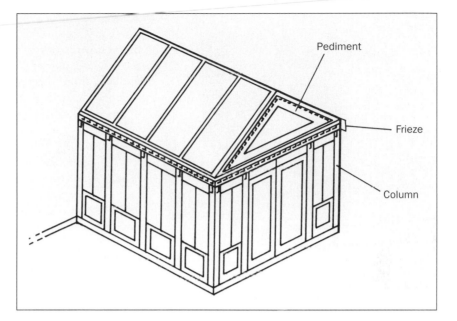

FIG. 30 The classical style.

FIG. 31 (OPPOSITE) Some designers would call this an Edwardian style. (Amdega Ltd)

with pediments typify this style. The roofs usually have a steeper pitch and the elevations should be as symmetrical as possible. This style is well-suited to orangeries, which have panels of wood or brick between the windows.

Georgian/Edwardian

These tend to be square or rectangular in shape, sometimes hipped, although not always, with an emphasis on the vertical by making the windows tall and narrow. Georgian, Edwardian and Regency all seem to be interchangeable.

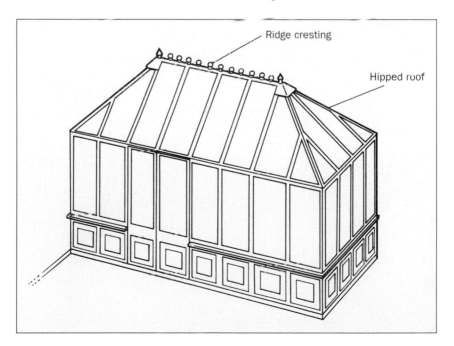

FIG. 32 Edwardian/ Georgian style.

FIG. 33 One of many designs in the Victorian style. (Rutland County Ltd)

FIG. 34 The Victorian style.

Victorian

The big problem with categorizing this style is that the Victorians borrowed freely from the past and their buildings combined all kinds of designs and features from history. In conservatory terms, 'Victorian' usually means octagonal bays, with plenty of ornate decoration and steeper pitches.

Contemporary

Any design that uses modern materials, or traditional ones in a modern way, tends to be called 'contemporary'. It is perfectly possible to add a modern-style conservatory to any kind of house and get a good-looking end result, provided it is well-designed and is sensitive to the surrounding architecture. To get a contemporary design, you will have either to contact one of the few suppliers who design and make them, or employ an architect to design one for you.

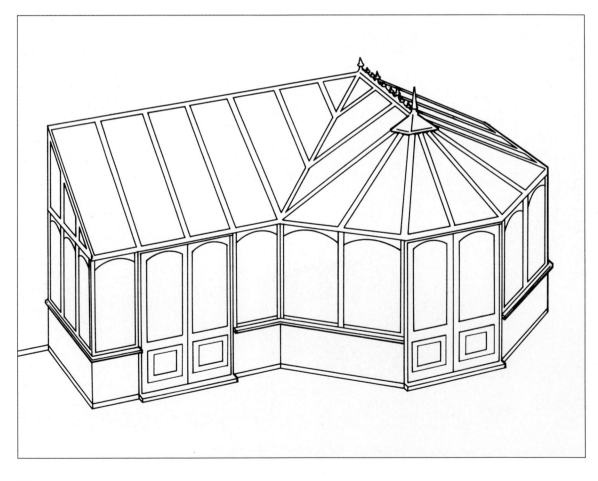

FIG. 35 *An uncompromisingly modern design. (Bartholomew Conservatories)*

FIG. 36 (OPPOSITE) Glass can look very dramatic if used in an imaginative way. (Bartholomew Conservatories. Architect: Hendy & Legge. Photographer: Eric Ellington)

FIG. 37 A contemporary style with an overhang to shade the sun. (Apropos Clear Span. Photographer: Hugh Palmer)

THERMAL GAIN

One of the most important features of your conservatory design is its relationship with the sun. Unfortunately, there are many misconceptions and much misinformation floating around. So to start with, whatever you have been told or read, a wall that faces due south is not the best place to build a conservatory. You should only do this if there are no other options and then you must make sure that you have enough in your budget to pay for the extras necessary to make such a space usable.

If a conservatory faces south, it will have the sun on it most of the day in summer, as well as late spring and early autumn and it will get too hot to sit in comfortably. Far too many people pay out a lot of money for a room that is too hot when the weather is sunny and too cold when it isn't. It is worth gaining

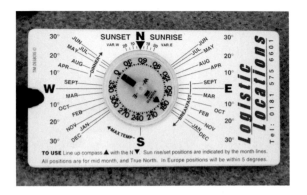

FIG. 38 *If you want to get an exact prediction of the angle and direction of the sun on any day of the year, use a sun-finding compass like this one.*

an understanding of the process by which heat builds up in conservatories, because it gives some important clues as to how to site and design a conservatory in order to minimize the problem. Most people have heard of the 'greenhouse effect' in relation to the climate and it works in a similar way on a much smaller scale for buildings with a lot of south-facing glass.

Radiant heat from the sun passes through the transparent glass into the conservatory, where it reaches the wall, floor and contents of the room. These absorb the heat and warm up. As they do so, they radiate heat themselves and heat up the air around them. This form of heat cannot pass back through the glass and so it becomes trapped in the space, increasing the temperature. The heat that builds up is called 'solar gain'. In this way, the conservatory can heat up to over 38°C (100°F) in the summer, if no remedial measures are taken. Humans start to feel uncomfortable at levels over about 25°C, so it is not hard to see why a conservatory in summer can become such an unpleasant place to be. The worst case is that it will only be at a tolerable temperature for around two hours per day, in the morning before the heat starts to build up. Unless you want a greenhouse to grow exotic plants that crave this kind

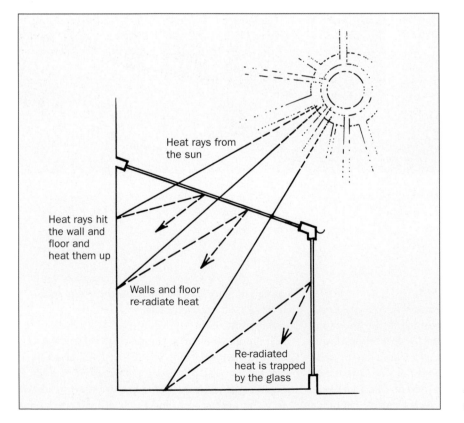

Heat rays from the sun

Heat rays hit the wall and floor and heat them up

Walls and floor re-radiate heat

Re-radiated heat is trapped by the glass

FIG. 39 *The greenhouse effect.*

FIG. 40 *Fans are a useful feature to help occupants feel cool in a conservatory that faces south. (Holloways Conservatory Furniture & Garden Ornament. Photographer: Bob Challenor)*

of environment, facing a glass box towards the sun is not a good idea.

In winter, the very poor insulating abilities of glass mean that lots of heat is allowed to escape. Even if the conservatory faces south, the solar gain is unlikely to compensate and the space will be too cold – below the 17°C that humans require to be comfortable without putting on extra clothing. If you look at the number of hours throughout the year that a south-facing conservatory can provide a temperature of between 17 and 25°C, it is actually less than the number of hours that a north-facing conservatory can provide. Although the latter does not benefit much from solar gain in the winter, in the summer, it is sheltered from much of the fierce heat of the sun and can be occupied without discomfort for much of the day. On balance, the best orientation is probably to face south-east because the high-angle sun will not

strike the conservatory squarely and so it will be partly sheltered in the afternoon when the temperature of the air is at its hottest. Also it will warm up in the morning more slowly, due to the lower air temperature and having cooled down significantly overnight.

There are several ways in which you can counteract the greenhouse effect, apart from the obvious one of orientating the house to reduce solar gain. Effective ventilation will help to release the overheated air, especially if it is situated at low level as well as high level, since this sets up a current as the

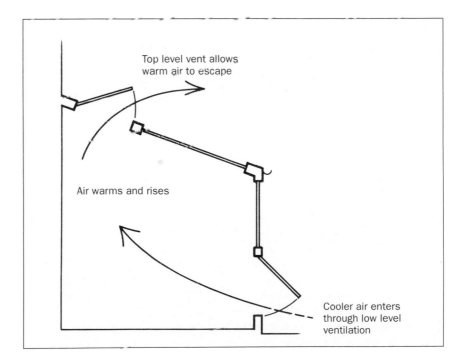

Top level vent allows warm air to escape

Air warms and rises

Cooler air enters through low level ventilation

FIG. 41 *Using ventilation to reduce solar gain.*

FIG. 42 Blinds can shelter a conservatory from the worst of the midday sun. (Oak Leaf Conservatories Ltd)

heat rises, even if there is no breeze. However, low-level windows or louvres are a security risk and a nuisance to keep opening and closing. The process can be mechanized to happen at the touch of a button, or even connected up to a temperature sensor that will adjust them for you. Solar reflective blinds will reduce the glare from the sun, but if they are inside they will not make a huge difference to the overall heat build-up, except to concentrate it in the gap between the frame and the glass, with a consequent risk of heat damage to lower-quality framing systems. Blinds are far more effective if they can be outside, or within the double-glazing units – both

relatively expensive options. They make most difference when fitted on the roof. In a similar way, solar control films can be applied to the glass to reduce the level of radiant heat getting in. Some are more effective than others, so if one is needed, it is worth investigating the types available and comparing alternatives. Another more exotic way to improve comfort during high summer is to include a small fountain or water feature, if the area is big enough.

There is an alternative strategy to dealing with heat gain in a conservatory – that is, to make use of the 'free heat' that it can provide and use this to lower your fuel bills. It can be used as a buffer zone on cool

44

but sunny days, to pre-heat the air before it enters the main house. This is particularly effective if several of the windows to other rooms open on to it, but you can close doors to seal it off from the rest of the house. If used as an entrance porch the conservatory plays an added role as a draught lobby and airlock, reducing heat loss from the house. If you want to accentuate these benefits, the conservatory should be run along as much of the masonry wall of the house as possible and the floor and walls should be a dark tone, which will absorb heat more readily than a lighter colour. Some keen environmentalists take it a step further and make the conservatory two stories high, so that the warmer air can be directed into the upper floors, consequently improving the air circulation and transfer of the heat into the house. There are some sophisticated systems that collect the heat and store it in a 'heat sink' – typically a swimming pool – to be used later to heat up water or space heating. If you want to maximize the 'free heat' benefits and minimize unnecessary waste of heat, a heating system should not be installed and the conservatory should not be used on cold days, except for storage. Also single-glazing is better for this approach, which means that the conservatory will have to be designed so that it is not covered by the Building Regulations (see later).

HEATING

The Building Regulations, and for that matter good management of the household finances, suggest that conservatories should not be heated other than by the natural ways mentioned earlier. This is because glass is very bad at keeping in heat and just adding a radiator attached to the central heating system will significantly raise your annual energy bill. So at an early stage you need to be clear whether you intend to create a space only for use on the warmer days of the year or if the conservatory is to be an all-year-round

FIG. 43 A double-height conservatory can act as a buffer between the house and outside. (Lisa Moth for Vale Garden Houses Ltd)

space that must be heated when it is cold. If it is to be artificially heated this should be borne in mind by the designer, who should try to minimize the area of glass relative to its area, for example by locating the building at an internal corner of the house, to give it two or three sides of masonry. A solid floor rather than a timber one will also help to retain the heat. You should also have the heating system checked by a plumber before going too far along the line, because the extra demand may be too much for the system and a new boiler may be required.

If the conservatory has to be heated, extending an existing gas-fired central heating is probably the cheapest method to use, but independent thermostatic control is essential, that is, a valve that will switch off the radiator when the temperature in the conservatory is at the chosen level. This will allow you to give the conservatory a boost relative to the rest of the house when it is cold. Also, you must be able to turn the heating off when the space is not being used, or it will carry on blasting heat and your money literally out of the window. Make sure that a CORGI-registered plumber carries out the work and that the building work is carefully planned and co-ordinated to hide as much of the pipework as possible. Positioning of the radiators in the room can be a challenge, especially if

FIG. 44 Conservatories lose a lot of heat in winter. (Oak Leaf Conservatories Ltd)

most of the walls are glass, but this problem can be overcome with long, low radiators or, ideally, perimeter heating, concealed at skirting level.

Another popular alternative is an electric portable oil-filled radiator, which is less expensive to buy but a lot more expensive to run. Other variants on the free-standing theme are LPG (gas) heaters that are portable and have a quicker response time than electricity, but can cause condensation. Open fires and wood-burning stoves are an attractive feature, with the added benefit that you are unlikely to go to the trouble of starting one up unless the room is going to be occupied, which avoids the expensive exercise of heating a room from the main boiler automatically regardless of how much it is used. However, a proper flue and chimney will be required and this will need to be carefully designed to avoid it becoming an eyesore. The chimney cannot just go straight through the glass or polycarbonate roof because neither of these is sufficiently heat resistant and there must also be a permanent supply of fresh air into the room via an airbrick or fixed grille.

Underfloor heating is sometimes used in conservatories, particularly because it gets around the problem of unsightly radiators, but it is most effective in a space that is going to be used regularly. An electric underfloor system is much more expensive to

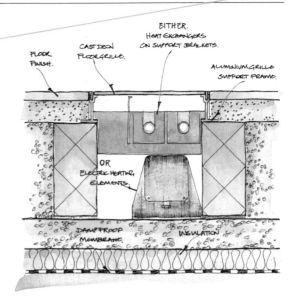

FIG. 45 *An underfloor heating system. (Lisa Moth for Vale Garden Houses Ltd)*

run than a wet system, but is cheaper to install if all the other rooms in the house are to remain on a conventional radiator system. Air conditioning is the most expensive option and should be avoided – it will never be effective unless you are prepared to pay a small fortune to run it. An attractive and traditional

FIG. 46 *A floor grille for an underfloor heating system. (Lisa Moth for Vale Garden Houses Ltd)*

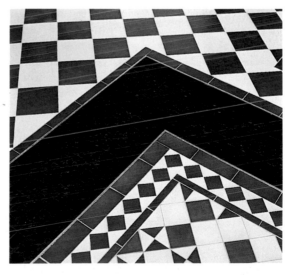

FIG. 47 *Here the grille has become part of the floor design. (Lisa Moth for Vale Garden Houses Ltd)*

way to heat a conservatory is to set grilles into the floor and run either heating pipes or an electric heat element below them.

You can help your heating system out a bit by fitting blinds, which will reduce heat loss when drawn at night, but are of limited use in the day, unless you want to sit in the gloom. There are various special coatings that can be applied to the glazing to reflect the heat back into the room and reduce heat loss when it is cold. However, an unwelcome effect of these coatings is that they may also exacerbate solar gain in the summer. Anti-stratification fans can be used in winter to recirculate the newly heated warm air that tends to rise and collect in the roof, whilst providing some air flow in summer.

CONDENSATION

When moist air meets a cool surface, water condenses on to it. Most homeowners, particularly if they only have single-glazed windows, are familiar with the unpleasant results of this effect in a house. Many of the things that we do in our homes produce moisture, such as washing and cooking and every one of us puts moisture into the air by breathing and sweating. Older properties with poorly fitting windows and chimneys offer plenty of routes for ventilation to remove the humid air. Modern buildings, with draught-proof windows and doors and central heating do not allow air to circulate to the same degree and consequently the amount of water vapour held in the air can build up to much higher levels. Moisture will form on the coldest surface first and in a house this is usually on the glass in the windows and the conservatory. So even if the conservatory is not a moisture-producing room like a kitchen or utility room, some of the air from these spaces will eventually find its way there. Condensation, especially if it is persistent, can cause long-term problems. A build-up of mould on the glass, walls and blinds can develop and if unchecked some types of furniture and fittings will rot. A conservatory suffering from excessive condensation will smell dank and feel clammy.

Condensation problems are more likely shortly after construction, particularly in winter. This is because most traditional building techniques leave water retained in the structure that can take many months to dry out – up to twelve months in some cases. Until the structure is dry, it will be releasing a steady flow of moisture that evaporates into the room. So it is important to keep the doors open as often as possible in the first few weeks after completion, and to monitor the situation and use a dehumidifier for a while if necessary.

Chronic condensation problems can be tackled in two ways. These are most effective if they are incorporated into the design (and budget) at an early stage, rather than waiting until the building has been finished and having to take remedial action.

The first weapon in the armoury is to increase the insulating capacity of the glazed roof and walls, because the warmer they are the less moisture they will collect. Double-glazing helps, but its surface temperature is still quite a lot lower than the main walls of the house. One of the Low-E glasses such as Pilkington K glass will improve things a little. For the roof, 25mm polycarbonate will insulate better and greatly reduce the condensation risk.

The other way to combat condensation is to increase the ventilation through the house and conservatory. In its simplest form, this involves opening windows and doors, but this is not practical all the time, so other steps that are more manageable are needed.

Before anything else, the level of moisture in the air for the whole house should be reduced at source, by ensuring that the kitchen, utility room and all the bathrooms have mechanical extracts that are sufficiently powerful and effective. Fitting extract fans with automatic control will improve the atmosphere in the whole house, as well as reduce the condensation risk on the glazing. In the conservatory itself, there should at least be windows at a high level that can be fixed open without compromising the security of the house when occupied. As mentioned earlier, these are of limited effect, unless there is some form of low-level ventilation as well, or air movement through the house to get a good air current running. If possible, roof vents should be fitted, either to be operated with a pole or electrically powered. These need to be carefully designed and built, though, to ensure that they are well-fitted and that there are no leaks. The opening area of roof vents should be about

FIG. 48 *High-level vents are used to help air flow through the building.*
(Lisa Moth for Vale Garden Houses Ltd)

10 to 15 per cent of the floor area. For a quicker effect, mechanical extracts can be mounted in the roof area, to pull air through the space at a much faster rate than might happen naturally, but these can be relatively noisy.

Apart from opening and closing windows or using mechanical means that set up noticeable air currents, it is also necessary to have a certain amount of background or 'trickle' ventilation. The idea of trickle vents is that they serve to replace the ventilation that resulted from the old-fashioned draughts in a house which have now been eliminated by modern construction methods. These vents are now a requirement of the Building Regulations and whenever a

49

new window is fitted they have to have an adjustable ventilation grille along the top. The idea is that they can allow permanent background ventilation to occur, keeping the air refreshed without a noticeable draught or compromising security. These are a huge benefit to the comfort of a conservatory, along with a ridge that is designed to do a similar job.

MAINTENANCE

Conservatories require more maintenance than other parts of a typical house. Not least, the window cleaning required will increase dramatically. Some materials will need more looking after than others. For example, a painted timber frame will need attention every three or four years to keep it in good condition. If it is stained, it will probably need retreating every five or six years. PVCu only needs an occasional clean down, but over many years in sunlight will start to discolour and then it too will require repainting. PVCu manufacturers may dispute this, but the paint supply companies now produce a range of products especially for this purpose, so someone must be using them.

When you are deciding on the location and design of the conservatory, the maintenance implications should be considered. If you are close to trees or have a bird table, droppings on the roof and windows will need to be cleaned off regularly. Trees will also shed their leaves on to the roof and into the gutter. A steeper roof may help, but sooner or later someone will have to get up there and clean it down. How easily and safely can a ladder be leant against the gutter? Once up to roof level is it possible to access the whole roof safely to clean it? The answer to the latter is often 'no', so wipers on poles are necessary. Sometimes it is possible to design the roof so that parts can be reached from upper-storey windows. If there is to be a valley between the existing structure and the conservatory, it could be made wider and strengthened so that someone can walk along it safely and reach the furthest part of the roof that way. Depending on the design of windows in the roof it may be possible to clean parts of the roof from these.

There is a risk that occasionally snow and loose tiles will fall from the main roof on to the fragile conservatory roof, causing damage. A snow guard to the edge of the house roof should hold back most of the snow. Regular maintenance of the main roof will lessen the risk of damage by falling tiles, or a stronger glass could be used for the roof of the conservatory.

FIG. 49 Steep roofs are easier to keep clean. (Durabuild Glazed Structures Ltd)

FIG. 50 Good daylight levels are guaranteed. (Holloways Conservatory Furniture & Garden Ornament. Photographer: Bob Challenor)

DAYLIGHT AND LIGHTING

There is a certain degree of expectancy with a conservatory. It should feel light, airy and bright and in most cases it will be, but if it is hemmed in by surrounding buildings or landscaping the effect will be the reverse and there is a possibility that you will end up emphasizing a small and cramped space. As a general rule, the more sky you can see from the space, the brighter the daylight level will be. If you have no choice on location you can reduce the negative effect by painting external brick walls a light colour, using a lighter colour floor, or cutting back or removing vegetation as much as possible.

Before designing the artificial lighting scheme, think about what you will be doing in the room. Different activities require different lighting levels and different qualities of light. For example, in an area where people are mainly sitting down and reading they will need accessible, bright lights that they can adjust. This suggests free-standing standard lamps or wall-mounted downlighters. If dinner parties are a major occurrence you need an average level of light, evenly distributed, ideally with dimmers for a more intimate feel. If the conservatory will be used for home working by you and for homework by the kids, you will need desk lamps and will not want low-level lights that create glare on a computer screen. The way to keep a space flexible is to fit two or three lighting schemes, which can be used to suit different situations. It is possible to obtain programmable lighting controls that will adjust the brightness of all the lights to pre-set patterns depending on need. A cheaper way is just to ensure that there are plenty of electrical sockets at various levels and use several types of independent and free-standing light fittings that can be moved around.

There are limited places on which to fix lights on conservatory walls, so it is a good idea to keep at least one masonry wall with enough uninterrupted surface area for this purpose.

Tip
A neat way of dealing with the clutter of having a central pendant light and a fan mounted on the ceiling is to combine them in one fitting.

SECURITY

It has to be said that conservatories are a potential weak spot in the security of a private house. They allow their contents to be visible, as well as the occupants (or lack of them). It is easier and less obtrusive to break through a sheet of glass than a normal wall. Moreover, conservatories are usually round the back, on the ground floor level and in a location chosen for privacy, so all the windows and doors must have good, secure locks. You should make an assessment of the level of security you think you will require, which will be partly based on the value of your house and contents and partly the crime rate in your area. Check your house contents insurance policy to ensure that you do not invalidate it by an inferior specification for security locks and alarms.

The existing alarm system should be extended. If there is not one, consider a smaller conservatory to pay for one to be installed – it will greatly reduce your chances of being burgled or will at least limit the amount stolen if someone does get in. Ideally, all windows and doors that can be opened should have alarms contacts and the whole room should be covered by a PIR (infra-red movement detector). Don't forget that vents need to be secure as well. Sometimes access is gained by removing poorly made louvres from their frame. If the conservatory has one of the stronger roof designs and it is at a shallow enough angle, an agile burglar could climb up and use it to access the upstairs windows, so make sure that these are also checked for their security and have window locks on as well.

If you have any doubts or concerns about the security that is proposed for your conservatory, get in touch with your nearest police station and ask for some of their leaflets and, if possible, your local crime prevention officer to visit. They will provide unbiased, expert advice on how to make your whole house secure, as well as the new addition you are planning.

TOWN VERSUS COUNTRY

The character of the area that your house is in may have a fundamental effect on the design. In tight urban spaces, where houses are cheek-by-jowl, space to extend in any kind of way will be at a premium.

52

The garden will be overlooked, so a transparent roof projecting too far out may allow the neighbours a view straight in, so obscured glass or polycarbonate will be needed. The local authority planners may place more restrictions on the size to avoid imposing on your neighbours. Many urban houses are narrow, with a deep plan, which makes a conservatory an ideal way to extend without losing valuable daylight from the centre. The spaces around the house are not likely to get much sun, which will be cut out by the closely packed buildings. They are likely to be small and paved, so the conservatory itself may also have to serve as a surrogate garden.

The many restrictions that are imposed in these locations mean that specialist designers really come into their own. A skilled designer can turn an awkward, potentially unappealing space into a bright and attractive area that enhances the appearance of the house and its surroundings.

One creative way to use a conservatory in an urban situation is to add it on the first floor, with either a masonry or glazed ground floor.

In villages and the countryside, there are more possibilities for exploiting one of the prime assets of a conservatory – that it can maximize the benefits of a good view. The garden is likely to be bigger and therefore will allow a larger footprint, or even a completely detached building. (A footprint is an area enclosed on the ground by a line drawn round the outside face of the extended walls of the house.)

WHO WILL BUILD IT?

Even at the design stage you need to have a good idea whether you will be using professionals or building the conservatory yourself, not least because of the effect that it will have on your budget. Unless you are particularly accomplished or determined when it comes to DIY, you will want a design that will be easy to build. That means keeping the shape simple and the size manageable. In fact, if you want to take on the assembly yourself it is not a bad idea to select the manufacturer as early as possible and make sure that it is within your capabilities. The fewer trimmings,

FIG. 53 There are many different ways to add a conservatory on to a flat wall.

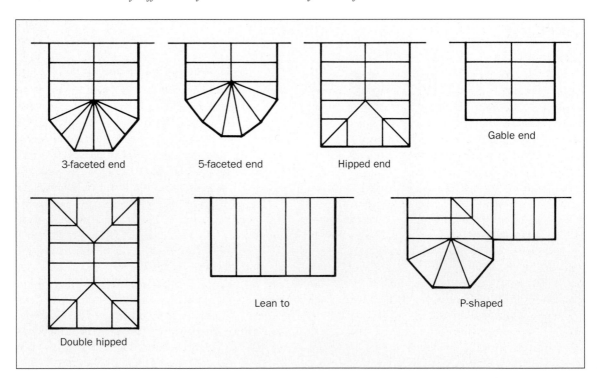

3-faceted end

5-faceted end

Hipped end

Gable end

Double hipped

Lean to

P-shaped

FIG. 54 With some houses, the only way to get it looking right is to use the same material and pitch as the main house. (Solarlux Systems Ltd, sliding & folding door systems)

changes of angle and awkward junctions with the masonry walls, the easier (and quicker) it will be to build.

WHERE SHOULD IT GO?

Sometimes the location of a conservatory is easy to decide. Once you know the size that you need or can afford, it may simply be a case of adding it on to the back of your house. But often there is some choice about the shape and position and how it can relate to the existing spaces, inside and out, especially if there is other building work going on in the house at the same time.

The relationship with the garden is a good starting point. Plant lovers will want to use the new microclimate that is created to grow some of the less hardy plants that wouldn't survive outside. Others will want to experience sitting in the garden without the inconvenience of the British weather. In these cases, the conservatory is really a modification of the garden rather than an extension of the house. Ideally, the garden should be redesigned at the same time, to ensure that the two spaces relate to each other properly. Many people take the opportunity to introduce a patio area, or a terrace, which is accessible from

some of the other rooms of the house, which it effectively links together in the summer. It may be worth starting with the kind of plants that are wanted, inside and out, and then planning the building and landscaping work to create the best possible conditions for them. This approach should filter down into the kind of materials and fittings that are to be used – for example, continuing the quarry tiles in the conservatory on and out into the garden. The reverse applies if the strongest tie is to be with the house, although some materials that are quite at home in your living room will not endure the temperature swings and higher humidity found under glass.

If there are trees or high bushes in your garden or the neighbouring gardens, they may significantly cut down the sunlight and daylight that reaches the conservatory, and so this needs to be included in any assessment of the best location. The shade may actually be an asset where the location is south-facing, but a disadvantage if it cuts off some of the little bit of sunlight that will reach a north-facing position. Privacy is also likely to be important and if the garden is overlooked or on the front of the house and visible from the road, you may accept the situation or use blinds, although a better way is to use screens of solid walls and obscured glass as part of the design. If

FIG. 55 (ABOVE) This design has copied the proportions of the main house, so that even though it is clearly an addition, it fits in. (Lamwood Ltd)

FIG. 56 Two separate parts of the house linked by a new conservatory. (Amdega Ltd)

you are going to keep valuable items such as computers in the conservatory, they should be well screened from view for security reasons.

As has been already stressed, the hardest part of designing a conservatory is avoiding the 'bolted-on' look. As well as a careful choice of style, getting the connection to the existing house right is crucial to success. The easiest way to connect new with old is to butt the conservatory up to flat masonry walls. This is because the joint can easily be cloaked with flashing, which serves to protect it from the weather. This junction is the commonest source of leaks, where two different structures and materials join (see Chapter 6 for how to do this properly).

Joining a glass or polycarbonate roof directly on to a typical tiled roof is difficult to build and will not look good, so if the conservatory is higher than the roof as in the case of a bungalow, either the existing wall and roof have to be built up, or the conservatory design has to be changed to a shallow monopitch that can be squeezed under the line of the eaves.

If the conservatory is to be part of other building works, there is a far better chance of ensuring that it looks integrated into the house. Rather than sticking it up against an existing straight wall, it may be possible to slot it in as a link between two sections of the house, or put it in an internal corner. Ideally, the conservatory roof should be a similar pitch to the main roof of the house, although cost and the tendency of it to clash with existing first-floor windows often prevent this from being an option.

Another aspect of the relationship between the existing house and its new addition is the new pattern of circulation through them both that will

FIG. 57 A neat join that looks like it has always been there. (Lamwood Ltd)

develop. Unless the conservatory is connected on to a convenient corridor or hall, you will have to go through one of the existing rooms to get to the conservatory and then pass through the conservatory to get to the garden. The corridor you walk through is one aspect of the design you may wish to consider. There may be all kinds of reasons why it is impossible to avoid having a central corridor with furniture either side of it. However, you may be able, for example, to place the door providing access from the conservatory to the garden on the left-, or right-hand, side of the conservatory, thus providing a circulation route which takes up less space and which enables you to have a better layout.

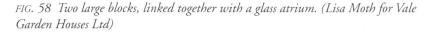

FIG. 58 Two large blocks, linked together with a glass atrium. (Lisa Moth for Vale Garden Houses Ltd)

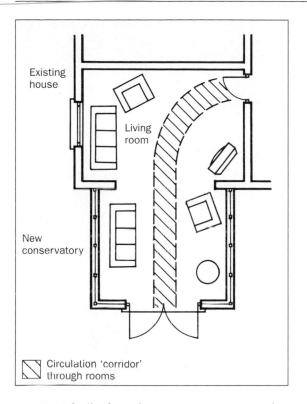

FIG. 59 A badly planned conservatory may waste a lot of space, which has to be given up to circulation.

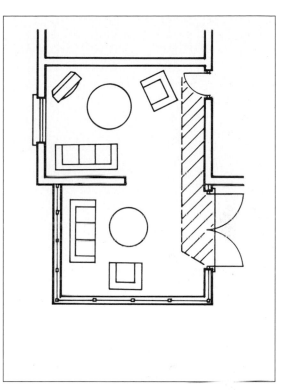

FIG. 60 This plan reduces the circulation area and the rooms have a better layout.

USES OF A CONSERVATORY

Most conservatories, like other rooms in the modern house, have more than one function. They are inherently flexible spaces, particularly if the shape is kept simple and the finishes are hard-wearing. But unlike the other rooms, the space will have a different feel at different times of the year. The changes in temperature, humidity and daylight levels that occur as the seasons change will be far more obvious; the conservatory will therefore probably be used in different ways according to the time of year. It is somehow much easier to sit there for breakfast on a bright sunny morning in June than sit in the cool gloom at the same time of day in December. In some cases, especially if it is not permanently heated, the conservatory will be closed down and used for storage by late autumn and will be in hibernation until the warmer weather returns in the spring. It will

also become the repository for all the garden furniture and other clutter that is also redundant over winter!

As part of the design process, you will need to decide what the primary uses of the conservatory are going to be. In the early stages, it is a good idea to try to keep an open mind and look at the house as a whole. Draw up a list of the extra space that you think you need, but don't just assume that the conservatory will cater for this use – see whether a better solution could be implemented, perhaps by altering the uses of the existing rooms. For example, if you need a bigger kitchen, rather than expanding it into a rear conservatory, you could instead use the new space as a family room/dining area and add the existing dining room on to the kitchen. Many modern families rarely use a separate dining room, which is kept for formal dinner parties that hardly happen. But an informal eating area attached to the

FIG. 61 *Plenty of plants blur the distinction between inside and outside. (Holloways Conservatory Furniture & Garden Ornament. Photographer: Bob Challenor)*

kitchen with a good view of the garden will be used virtually every day.

Here are just a few suggestions as to how conservatories can be used to add to the quality of life in your home.

Garden Room

Plants are, after all, what conservatories were invented for and there is no doubt that they provide a lot of exciting opportunities for plant lovers to extend the range of their repertoire. They are also an excellent place to cultivate seedlings. There is a wide range of plants that can be grown and there are plenty of sources of reference which explain how to use your conservatory successfully as a part-time greenhouse. If it is designed to relate well to the landscaping around it, a conservatory can extend your enjoyment of the garden across the seasons. Indoor plants must be carefully chosen and managed to suit the microclimate. Control of the temperature and the flexibility of the heating system are also crucial, since the temperature will have to be regulated carefully over

each twenty-four-hour period as well as having to deal with the changes in the climate outside. Humidity must be kept high for many plants, which is difficult to maintain under glass in the UK summer, especially if you go away on holiday, as it can involve spraying plants regularly, or leaving trays of water around.

Family Room

This is a very popular use for conservatories, utilizing their flexibility to the full. They are ideal places for small children to play, with more durable finishes and fittings than the rest of the house; even a paint tin, which is traditionally dropped on the floor at least once a week by a toddler, will not cause a disaster. Conservatories are often connected to the kitchen, which tends to be where the adult supervising the toddler is most likely to be found during the day. In order to comply with regulations, the glass in the windows and doors of the conservatory must be toughened or laminated, to avoid the risk of injury if the glass is bumped into during boisterous play.

Older kids can use the space to play with friends or do their homework; parents can sit there to relax and read the paper. There is plenty of light during the day for reading, although blinds are essential to make this activity comfortable when the sun shines in. Conservatories are ideal for gatherings with friends – again, this works well if there is a direct link with the kitchen, for informal meals.

If a hi-fi is to be installed, or parties are to be held, remember that the impression that a conservatory is merely another part of the house is an illusion in terms of sound insulation. Glass is just as poor at keeping sound in as it is at retaining heat and loud noise – the enhanced bass of modern speakers, or roars of laughter from happy guests, will travel far and wide. If you are in close proximity to your neighbours, you should avoid any noisy activities in the conservatory in the late evening. TV is also a potential source of night-time disturbance to your neighbours. When siting a TV, as with a computer monitor, some careful thought is needed so that the

sun is not shining on the picture, nor directly behind it, nor is reflected back at the viewer from the screen.

Given the range of things that will go on in a family room, it should be planned with some thought given to what furniture will be needed and also where the storage that will inevitably be required will be created. The fittings and finishes must be robust, but this aesthetic is very suitable for a conservatory anyway.

Kitchen

Enlarging the existing kitchen is often the starting point that spurs homeowners on to acquire a conservatory, although it is not necessarily the ideal situation for the kitchen itself. Kitchens need a lot of storage, including cupboards at high level. Worktops have to be around 900mm above the floor level, which needs to be up against a wall with a sill that is at least 150mm higher. Neither of these requirements is particularly compatible with glass walls. Because of the cutting, chopping and food preparation that goes

FIG. 62 *Toplight is useful in a kitchen, where good vision is essential for food preparation. (Apropos Clear Span. Photographer: James White)*

on, a good level of light is vitally important. This is fine during the day when the light levels will be excellent, but in the evening high levels of artificial light will be necessary and there are a limited number of places to fix lights on a standard glass or polycarbonate roof. Kitchens are also a major source of moisture in the home and, as noted earlier, moist air and glass is not a good mix. This is especially so in winter when you will not want to lose heat by opening roof vents or doors and windows, but the glass will be at its coldest and most ready to produce condensation.

All this is not to say that you should never put a kitchen in a conservatory. But if you do, the relative disadvantages have to be anticipated and dealt with. A specialist kitchen designer must be involved at an early stage and you must certainly have an acceptable layout worked out in detail before you finally place the order for the conservatory. At the same time, a strategy for dealing with the various moisture-producing activities should be developed. Cooker hoods can incorporate an extractor fan and you don't have to go for the minimum rate of air changes required by the regulations. The quicker and more efficiently the humid air can be removed, the less chance there is for it to find its way to the glass where it can condense and start to form drips of water. Unless condenser models are used, the washing machine should be located somewhere else, such as in a utility room, along with the dryer and the dishwasher if possible. Any wall-mounted extractor fan

FIG. 63 Kitchens need wall space for cupboards. (Bartholomew Conservatories)

FIG. 64 An elegant space in which to dine. (Lisa Moth for Vale Garden Houses Ltd)

should be positioned near to the area generating the moisture to avoid pulling it across the room and dispersing the water vapour. Those who are conscious of the energy wasted may wish to use a more sophisticated extractor system that incorporates a heat exchanger to harvest the heat out of the air and use it to warm up fresh air coming through an intake. Generally, wet clothes should not be hung out in the conservatory kitchen, but taken to a separate area to dry.

The cupboard units can either be arranged in an island-type design if there is space, or the conservatory should be designed so that there are some masonry walls to fit them on to. Lighting can be built in to the underside of the cupboard units, or fixed to the ridge.

Access to kitchens is important since shopping, household goods and so on are regularly taken there from the outside. It is not ideal to have to circulate through another room such as the living room, to get there from the outside. This may be necessary, since conservatories are usually added on to the outside of a house and there is often another room between them and the main hall, but access from a garden path leading to the front of the house is a benefit if it can be arranged.

Dining Room

Conservatories are ideal places in which to entertain guests and eat. They can also be associated with the patio, where a barbecue can be set up on warmer days, or a garden table can be set up for dinner parties to decant to after the meal. A good use for a conservatory is to open out the side of a kitchen to form an associated informal dining area, separated by a half wall and connected to the outside by double doors. This maintains the connection with the kitchen, where food is being prepared and also allows plenty

FIG. 65 *Conservatories are a good place to entertain guests. (Holloways Conservatory Furniture & Garden Ornament. Photographer: Bob Challenor)*

FIG. 66 (BELOW) *A light, airy space in which to relax. (Lamwood Ltd)*

Tip

A fold-down or 'gate leg' table is a good space-saving device, which can be kept to one side out of the way until it is needed for a dinner party.

---

of light into it. Again, the layout needs to be considered at an early stage, the crucial factor here being the maximum number of guests who will need to be accommodated. Ideally, the actual table that is going to be used should be measured with chairs around it, to ensure that it will fit comfortably into the available space and will not interrupt circulation routes. In fact, during the daylight hours when the glazed walls give the illusion of more space than there actually is available, it is possible to squeeze a table and chairs into a smaller space than would be possible with a normal room, without it feeling cramped.

If the conservatory is to be used as a dining room, it is likely to be in use in the evenings when it is dark and so lighting is very important and should be designed in at an early stage. A particularly nice feature is a decorative central light that can be pulled down when needed. Cutlery, plates, napkins and so on will need to be stored somewhere and the plan should allow for the appropriate furniture to do this. If the area of the conservatory is going to be small

relative to the number of likely dinner guests, fit mechanical extracts in order to deal with the moisture and heat that will be generated, thereby keeping the conservatory free from fug and the guests awake by drawing fresh air in from outside or the rest of the house.

Living Room

One of the most common uses of a conservatory is to add an extra area of living room, often by enlarging an existing lounge and sometimes as a completely separate area in another part of the house. There are several factors that should be considered prior to designing such a space. If the new room is to be used at certain times of the day, this may affect its location. For example, if it is to be used in the evenings and there are young children in the house, it should be sited away from their bedrooms, to avoid any noise disturbing them. If it is an 'all day' space, it should relate closely to the other rooms of primary activity, such as the kitchen. If it is to be used to entertain guests, who may not always be close friends or family, it should be sited for easy access from the hallway, without having to go through the kitchen, perhaps walking past a pile of yesterday's dirty dishes, or the latest load of washing.

Since it is a space where people will be sitting and

FIG. 67 A multi-purpose room. (Rutland County Ltd)

admiring the view, it should also look out on to the better part of the garden and ideally have access to it as well. Comfortable chairs, settees and sofas as well as other furniture at the right level for people sitting in them, such as coffee tables, are essential. When people are sitting talking on a bright summer's day they may be grateful for blinds that reduce the worst of the glare, making it possible to look at people with the sun behind them without squinting. Good shade will also make reading easier on the eye.

Home Office

Whether a conservatory is the right place for a home office of any kind is debatable. Conservatories do not stand much clutter before becoming unattractive. The plethora of basic office equipment, such as files, books, telephones, computers and printers, plus all the related plugs, wires, debris and general bits and pieces generated by the working environment will quickly change a calm peaceful space into a chaotic room that can never be made to look quite tidy. There is also an argument that the conditions created under glass, which make conservatories so attractive in your hours of leisure, are actually a disadvantage for a work space. This environment is not conducive to the use of computers, since there is a conflict between monitors and any source of glare or significant background light. The temperature fluctuations make it less desirable as a space that has to be continually occupied, whatever the conditions, and making phone calls in a heavy rainstorm, talking over the sound of water hitting glass or plastic, is not easy. There may also be some implications for the security of your home if the conservatory is visible from the road. It is essential to let your insurers know and take out some kind of further insurance through your employer or business if you work from home regularly. Thieves are known to target home offices, due to the likelihood of finding laptops and other expensive equipment, and if they are all on show though the glass it will increase the risk of a break-in.

However, conservatories are a good place to use as an occasional working place. If you decide to use the conservatory in this way you can take several steps to reduce the disadvantages. Computer screens are best against a solid wall, so as to reduce the contrast between the screen and its surroundings. If there is a window or bright light source directly behind a screen, the eye struggles to adjust between the two levels and headaches can result after relatively short periods of use. Reflected light can cause a similar problem and solar blinds that will cut out a lot of the light are essential to stop it. There should also be a desk lamp available for reading and so on. Thermal comfort is very important to working well, so mechanical extracts and fans will be needed in the summer, along with good heating in the winter. A free-standing, mobile air-conditioning unit is ideal to position next to your desk during the hottest months.

If you are planning to work only occasionally in a room, it is tempting to make use of the usual domestic furniture, but this is not a good idea if you will be using it for more than an hour or two at a time. A desk at the proper height, with an adjustable chair, will help to reduce the risk of backache and other work-related injuries. If you employ anyone and expect them to come to your home to work, you will be answerable to the same health and safety legislation as a small office and will have a duty of care to do all of the things required by the regulations. It is possible to deal with the clutter created by office equipment by means of well-planned storage, adequate cupboards and drawers, along with pre-planned concealed routes for trunking to conceal power cables and telephone wires.

If your business is something with a more practical bent, involving tasks such as painting and illustrating or sewing, or any kind of work that requires good vision, then the conservatory will be the ideal place to work, provided that you can avoid direct sunlight.

FIG. 68 (OPPOSITE) A mix of wood, glass and steel form a perfect living room. (Bartholomew Conservatories. Architect: Jane Jones-Warner RIBA)

Hint

A good trick used by experienced homeworkers is to build a large cupboard, incorporating a computer, desk, shelves and drawers. When not in use, the chair is slid under the desk and the main cupboard doors are closed, concealing the whole workstation and restoring the domestic feel to the room.

Swimming Pool

Swimming pools are becoming more and more popular as additions to larger family homes. Unfortunately, given the British climate, there are some drawbacks to building an uncovered pool in the garden. They are unusable for many months of the year to all but the most hardy swimmers and have a tendency to collect insects, leaves and other dirt from the garden. However, domestic-sized pools can feel a bit cramped if they are enclosed as part of the house; covering them with a glass structure may therefore be the ideal solution. This will maintain contact with the outside and preserve the feeling of space and light, while also providing an environment suitable for use all year round. A conservatory allows the pool to open off the main house, and also protects it from the climate as well as garden debris.

Swimming pools are relatively large features and need a large structure to enclose them, at least 6m by 10m, allowing for the size of a typical pool plus space to walk around it. These dimensions can be reduced if the pool is the type that generates a current to swim against. Likewise, a glass roof over a swimming pool is a more ambitious affair than most other types of domestic conservatory. It will have to be designed to reach across a large span and will need support from a proper structural frame. There will have to be some effective ventilation and heating to keep the temperature acceptable, plus probably a dehumidifier to reduce the amount of condensation that may form on the roof (although drips are less of a problem in a pool, since the occupants are likely to already be quite wet). Ideal conditions should be created and maintained by using automatically controlled sensors. For those with bigger budgets, doors that fold or slide back to open up a whole side of the room could link the pool to the garden when the weather conditions permit and there are some sophisticated retractable systems that will allow the roof to be rolled back like the top of a convertible car.

All pools need a significant enclosed area for the filtration plant, pump and so on, which are unsightly and a source of noise and so must be housed in a solid masonry box. A toilet, shower and changing area are also needed, so a certain amount of traditional building work is unavoidable.

Links and Circulation Areas

Walls and roofs made of glass can be used very effectively to link up other rooms or to provide a route to connect together different parts of the house. A classic arrangement is to use the conservatory to join

FIG. 69 (OPPOSITE) A place in which to swim and relax. (Amdega Ltd)

FIG. 70 This design connects the house to the garden. (Lisa Moth for Vale Garden Houses Ltd)

FIG. 71 A conservatory for circulation and repose. (Durabuild Glazed Structures Ltd)

FIG. 72 Two parts of a house at 90 degrees to each other are joined by glass. (Quayside Conservatories Ltd. Architect: Scurr & Partners)

FIG. 73 A double-height conservatory extending over two levels of the house. (Glass Houses Ltd Photographer: Hugh Palmer)

together a living room, kitchen and dining area, with glazed double doors between them that can be folded back to make one large free-flowing space, which is both useful for parties and can also make a house feel bigger. If a long, potentially dark corridor is needed, the gloom can be relieved by using glazing for all or part of it, at the same time changing the floor and wall finishes accordingly. Existing rooms in the house that are not linked can be joined, perhaps by running a glazed 'lean-to' along the outside wall. A trick often used by architects when joining a new extension on to a particularly attractive, self-contained house, without the new addition detracting from the orig-

inal, is to join the two with a conservatory. This works particularly well where the extension design is radically different in character from the original. The conservatory acts as a transition between new and old. Conservatories are often deployed very successfully in this way for listed buildings or properties with a strong architectural personality.

Sometimes a floor on one level can be combined with circulation on another, which gives all kinds of opportunities for interesting designs, incorporating galleys, stairs and landings.

In a similar way, an entrance porch can be added on to a house without spoiling its proportion,

character and style. The visually lightweight appearance of glazed roofs and walls and contrasting construction will give a pleasing result where an ordinary masonry porch would look out of scale and incongruous. A conservatory in this location, when skilfully designed, can help to highlight and draw attention to the point of entry to the house for visitors, with the added benefit of providing a buffer against draughts without losing light into the hallway.

First-Floor Rooms

Conservatories do not make ideal bedrooms, because of the temperature swings, noise from rain and not least the greater level of privacy demanded. However, if the space is large enough, one end could be given a glazed roof and walls, particularly if an all-year-round balcony is wanted (perhaps as a sitting area). The latter can be screened off with curtains or a glazed screen to separate it from the main bedroom area and provide some privacy. Separate rooms can be created

over flat-roof single-storey extensions, to make use of areas that would otherwise be unusable space for most of the year. In these cases, a planning application will be necessary and the planning department will place restrictions on the location and which walls are glazed, in order to prevent neighbouring houses being overlooked. Because the first floor is more exposed to the elements than the relatively protected ground floor areas, good, robust construction detailing is important. The building regulations will require there to be at least one window with a low sill so that it can be used as a means of escape in the event of fire. If it is built onto an existing extension with an ordinary flat roof, at least the roof joists will need to be strengthened to bear the extra weight of furniture and people and structural improvements may even be needed to the ground floor walls as well. Generally speaking bathrooms do not fit comfortably into highly glazed spaces, but if it is unavoidable, full height blinds and very efficient heating and ventilation are essential.

FIG. 74 (OPPOSITE) An unusual and inventive first-floor conservatory. (Glass Houses Ltd. Photographer: Hugh Palmer)

FIG. 75 A balcony has been ingeniously formed from the conservatory to give a double benefit to this house. (Rutland County Ltd)

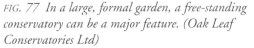

FIG. 76 (OPPOSITE) *An elegant free-standing gazebo. (Glass Houses Ltd. Photographer: Hugh Palmer)*

FIG. 77 *In a large, formal garden, a free-standing conservatory can be a major feature. (Oak Leaf Conservatories Ltd)*

Free-Standing

If you are fortunate enough to own a large garden, rather than build a conservatory next to or on to the house, you may choose to build a free-standing structure away from it, to form a gazebo. This is a wonderful addition to a landscape design, particularly if there are views that can be exploited.

THE SURVEY

Before design work can start in earnest, the area of the existing house to be extended should be thoroughly and accurately surveyed. Depending on who is providing your conservatory, this will either be carried out by a professional, or by yourself. It is vital

that this part of the job is done properly, because if something significant is missed and only discovered as the builders begin work there could be problems. It could lead to delays and unexpected costs, but the nightmare scenario is that the conservatory will not fit or is inappropriate in some way and has to be modified. The easiest way to avoid this, or at least to reduce the risk, is to use a company that will carry out a survey as part of their service to supply the conservatory. If the conservatory then does not fit, it will be their responsibility and they will have to put it right. Anything that is likely to influence the design and construction of the property needs to be noted and considered.

The existing house and surrounding part of the

garden should be measured up. This should include a check that walls are square to each other in plan and plumb. This is often not obvious to the eye alone, but the conservatory design may need to be adjusted accordingly. Precision-made conservatory frames are harder to adjust on site than brick walls. Any significant changes of level should also be noted, although these are usually easily absorbed by the foundation and brick base, which should be levelled off ready for the assembly of the frame. An appraisal should be made as to whether the planned building will fit comfortably in the space available, by marking it out on the ground. It's not just a question of whether there is room for it, but also whether the spaces left are adequate or of any use.

Which direction the sun comes from in relation to the site is a very important question, for reasons already explained earlier. But just as important is how much shade there will be from surrounding trees and buildings. Whether the conservatory will be overlooked by neighbours and how close the conservatory will be to neighbouring buildings and their boundaries should also be checked. Planning permission may be required depending partly on the size of the existing house and a calculation may be necessary (explained further in Chapter 4). Whilst looking at the existing house, any features that may have to be moved or adapted should be noted, such as meter boxes, boiler flues and airbricks that are ventilating floor voids. If any services such as water, gas and electricity will be affected, at some point an electrician or plumber will be needed to cap off or divert them. The existing drain runs should be noted, not least so that they can be used to drain the new roof if possible. If there are any drains that will be running under the new conservatory, these should be noted. Any manholes may have to be moved or kept, but they will need to be built into the new floor so that they can be identified. If a drain run is on the exact line of the foundations, it will have to be moved to one side.

Careful study of an existing older house may give useful clues. Cracks may reveal either poor ground or that the house must be treated cautiously when it comes to any building work. It is very difficult to tell just from looking at a building whether it has special foundations, or even that it has an unusual construction, such as a timber frame. If the house is relatively new, the construction can be checked by consulting the local authority building control records. A lot may be learned from neighbours who own a similar property and have already had building work carried out.

A professional surveyor or designer will also be thinking further ahead than the design stage, to the practical organization of the construction process and

FIG. 78 Manhole covers should be lifted to confirm the assumed direction of the drains.

how this may affect the cost. Builders will need access to the area of the work, ideally not through the house. If this has to happen, it will limit the size of digger and similar plant that can be used on the job and increase the disruption to the occupants. Storage space will be needed for at least a small amount of building materials, with ideally a secure place such as a garage to keep tools and other items vulnerable to theft. A skip will inevitably be needed and can be positioned on a typical suburban street, but may block a smaller private drive or shared forecourt

WORKING WITH A DESIGNER AND VISUALIZING THE END RESULT

However you eventually acquire your conservatory, at some point you will either have to sit down with a designer, or you will have to work out a design on your own. After preparing a brief, as described earlier, and having thought about how you might integrate it into your existing house, you then have to find a way of visualizing the end result. The professionals will have no trouble envisaging how the finished article will look and feel, but their mental picture is useless unless they can communicate it to you and your family. Do not be brushed off on this point by assurances from the experts that a design will suit your requirements. Their idea of what is acceptable or beautiful may be very different from your own. Don't place the order until you are entirely satisfied that it will fulfil your brief as much as possible for the money that you have available and that you have a clear idea of what it will look like.

There are several ways of achieving this objective. Firstly, you can look at photographss of similar projects, although you may find some companies only have a limited range of these, coupled with lots of information on the different conservatory shapes and designs in isolation. Viewing examples of a similar design or layout is obviously useful, but you need to gain a clear idea of how it might look in relation to your house, rather than alongside a lot of others in the showroom.

How will it suit the scale, style, proportion and material of the house to which it will be added? Will it be big enough? Will the furniture that you want

---

Checklist

The following should be checked at an early stage, before detailed designs are produced and costed:

- all critical dimensions
- that the walls are plumb and square in plan
- the levels of the surrounding garden
- the size in relation to the preferred design
- direction of the sun
- how shaded the site is
- whether Planning/Building Regulations applications may be needed
- any demolition requirements and how they will affect the occupants
- how existing services will be affected
- the existing drains
- the structure of the existing house
- whether any special construction will be required
- access for builders
- storage for materials.

---

put in it fit in a sensible way? CAD (computer-aided design) models can be helpful in these situations, especially when you are trying to work out layouts, although the cheaper software packages, which use unrealistic-looking 3D blocks, will not give a reliable image of how the design will actually look. The more skilled designers may be able to provide you with freehand sketches that can give a better impression of how the design will 'feel' to be in. Sophisticated computer techniques can be used to provide photomontages, which combine a photo of the house with a computer-generated image of the conservatory 'pasted' on to it. The high-end CAD systems can account for the direction of the sun and reflections of nearby objects, to give a very realistic picture of the finished building, but these kinds of resources are expensive and not generally available.

One low-technology technique available to anyone is to use some ordinary graph paper. Devise a scale, by counting each of the smallest squares as, say, 50mm, and draw on lines to indicate the main walls of the house in plan. Allow for the thickness of the individual walls if you want to be reasonably accurate. Then work out what furniture you expect to put into the conservatory, draw each one to the same

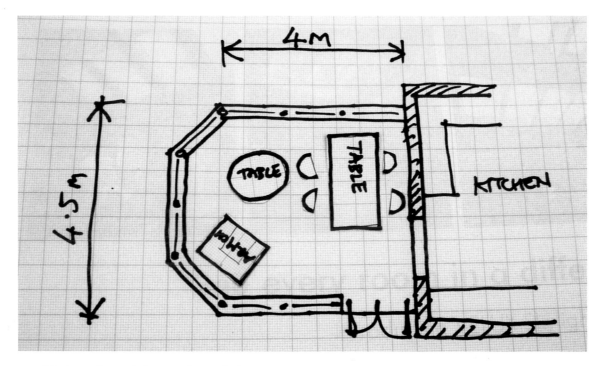

FIG. 79 Approximate designs can be roughed out using graph paper.

scale individually on a separate piece of graph paper and cut them out. Overlay your drawing of the house with a sheet of tracing paper and trace it off. Using catalogues to estimate standard dimensions of the walls, draw the approximate plan of your new conservatory, tracing through to gridlines below to get the scale correct. Then arrange the furniture cutouts on the new plan to see how it all goes together. You may have to do this several times before you get a layout that is suitable. If you can go through this simple process at the start of your project, you will be armed with a good idea of the size and possible cost of your conservatory before you start any detailed discussions with designers or sales representatives.

Once the design process is complete and you have

Tip

If you stake out your plan on the lawn, or chalk it on to the patio to appreciate its size in context, beware of the optical illusion that will make it appear smaller than it will be when complete. Try to view similar-sized conservatories to get an accurate appreciation of how the end result will feel.

---

a set of drawings that show you what you are about to order, pull out your original checklist. See how the design matches up to it – you may have modified your original ideas since the beginning, but it is useful to see how well you have achieved your original objectives. In 90 per cent of cases, the amount you are about to pay will be significantly more than you originally estimated.

CHAPTER 4

Dealing with Local Authorities

After you have settled on a design for your conservatory, have ensured that it is within your budget and are ready to provide the go ahead to the project, someone will have to check whether the approval of the local authority will be needed, and, if so, find out whether it will be forthcoming without requiring any alterations. In an architecturally sensitive neighbourhood, contact should be made with the planners at an early stage and any unusual construction should also be discussed with the Building Control Officer before assuming that it will be acceptable.

Usually, the planning authority in an area is the district or metropolitan council and the department involved will be called something like 'Development Control', 'Directorate of Community Development', 'Development Services' or some such similar title. This department is usually split into two sections, Planning and Building Control, which are actually quite separate functions. Some people confuse them when making an early enquiry and end up not being sure whether they have spoken to a Planning or Building Control Officer, so it is important to understand the difference.

A Planning Officer should not be offering advice on the Building Regulations and a Building Control Officer is not the best person to consult about planning restrictions. Just because one type of officer approves your design, it does not imply approval by the other. Although most councils will advise you if you need other types of approval, there is no law that says they have to – it is the responsibility of the owner of the property to ensure that everything is properly applied for and approved.

The consequences of not getting the proper approvals in place, if they are needed, are serious. Aside from the potential problems that can be caused by neighbours, solicitors routinely check that the paperwork is there when they do a search on behalf of a purchaser. Any omissions will significantly devalue a property.

THE PLANNING SYSTEM

The UK has one of the most regulated planning systems in the world, and if you get it drastically wrong the local authority can force you to demolish your conservatory. Fortunately, as long as some simple rules are followed and a dialogue is established with the Planning Officer early on, this nightmare scenario is not hard to avoid.

Do You Need Planning Permission?

Many conservatories quite simply do not need planning approval at all. This is because in ordinary residential areas that have no special planning controls, the government has decided that private homeowners should be allowed to make minor additions and alterations without going through the process of applying for and receiving planning permission. These are known as 'permitted development rights'.

Permitted development rights allow minor works within the boundary of a house, but these rights can only be used once after a house has been built, unless the alteration was made before 1948. So, for example, if your house had a significant extension in 1952, the rights allowed for it have probably been used up. There is a detailed description of everything that is allowed as permitted development in the

---

Permitted Development Rights for a Private Dwelling

If the following statements apply to your situation, you are unlikely to need Planning Permission:

- if your house is a terrace, or not in an area of special control and the conservatory is no more than either 10 per cent of the volume of the house, or 50cu m, whichever is the greater (but never more than 115cu m).

or

- if your house is semi-detached or detached, not in an area of special control and the conservatory is no more than 15 per cent of the volume of the house, or 70cu m, whichever is the greater (but never more than 115cu m)

and

- the conservatory does not come within 5m of an outbuilding; if it does, then the outbuilding is included as part of the extra volume being added to the house

and

- the roof isn't higher than the main roof of the house

and

- it isn't closer to a road than the house, or within 20m of a highway

and

- it isn't more than 4m high if it is within 2m to the boundary

and

- its area is not more than half of the total garden around the house

and

- there are no alterations to the roof of the house

and

- you are not in an area of special control such as a Conservation Area.

---

legislation, but only part of it is relevant to adding a conservatory.

AREAS OF SPECIAL CONTROL

If there are any special controls on the area that you live in, matters can become a little more complex. Examples of these are Conservation Areas, Listed Buildings, Areas of Outstanding Natural Beauty and Tree Preservation Orders. The planning authorities in the affected areas are given extra powers to control and restrict how buildings are altered and extended. If these restrictions apply, homeowners usually find out before they buy their house. If the restrictions are imposed after purchase, the owners may be informed as part of the consultation process beforehand, but not necessarily. If you are unsure whether there are any unusual planning controls, consult the planning authority, because there are heavy financial penalties if work is carried out without permission.

Conservation Areas

Conservation areas are designed to protect the character of groups of buildings and their surroundings, which are considered by the local council to have special architectural or historical interest. This means that the primary concern is the overall appearance of houses from the outside and the impact that any proposed alterations would have on the appearance of the street and surroundings. The effect of being in a Conservation Area is that the permitted development rights are reduced, or taken away altogether. If permitted development rights are maintained, the volume that you are allowed to add is reduced to 50cu m or 10 per cent of the existing volume, whichever is the greatest. Sometimes, these rights are removed altogether, which means that you will always need to obtain approval for your conservatory.

Having obtained these powers, the council will use them to control the design and materials used and it is highly unlikely that it will permit cheaper designs, or the use of less traditional materials such as PVCu. If the council considers that the siting of the conservatory is inappropriate for the form and scale of the existing house, it will refuse to allow it at all. Visibility is also important, so if the conservatory is discreetly tucked away behind the house and cannot be seen from the road, they will be more flexible. Even so, the cheapest conservatory allowable in a conservation area may cost more than the equivalent in a normal situation.

Listed Buildings

Buildings are listed by the government, which delegates the task to English Heritage, which in turn

Example of a Conservatory that Does not Need Planning Permission

- Location: an ordinary suburban street, of no special architectural or scenic value.
- House type: three bedroom semi-detached.
- House volume (including roof): 8m × 9m footprint, 440cu m.
- Conservatory size: 4m × 4m footprint, 52cu m.
- Conservatory location: back of a two-storey house.
- 15 per cent of 440cu m is 66cu m, but the greater of the two limits is allowed, so 70cu m is the maximum size before planning permission is needed. The conservatory will be 53cu m, which is well within this limit.
- There is a garage nearby, but it is not nearer than 5m after the conservatory has been built, so it will not be included when calculating the final volume of the extension. The conservatory will be around the back and so not near a road.
- The conservatory will be within 2m of the boundary, but will not be more than 4m high.
- There is a large garden, so the conservatory will not occupy more than half of the area of land surrounding the house.
- It will be a single storey on a two-storey house, so the main roof will not have to be altered.
- The area does not have any special planning controls.

Consequently, an application for Planning Permission will not be required.

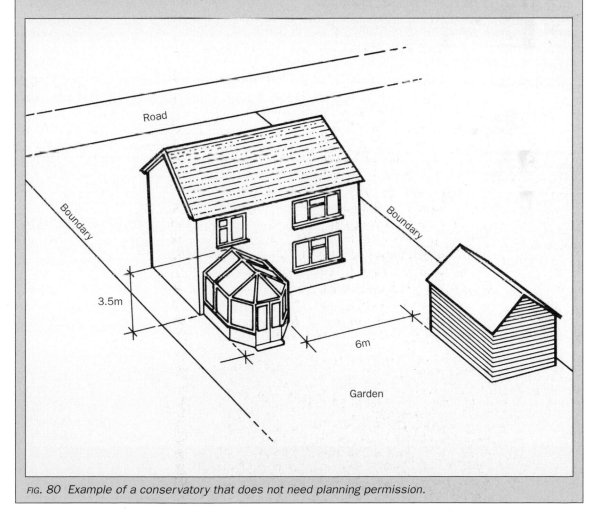

FIG. 80 Example of a conservatory that does not need planning permission.

81

monitors any alterations in conjunction with the local authority. To be listed, a building has to be of special architectural or historical interest and there are three grades. Most buildings are Grade II, a few are Grade II* and a few buildings, the most important, are designated Grade I. Unlike a property in a Conservation Area, the whole building, including the inside, is protected and also all structures within the boundary of the site. If you want to add a conservatory to a listed building, always seek expert advice – you will need a good-quality design and will have to put up a very convincing case to persuade the authorities that it will not adversely affect the appearance of the house. Altering any part of a listed building in any way, without express approval, is a criminal offence and can involve fines, plus orders to change the altered areas back to their original condition.

FIG. 81 (OPPOSITE) The local authority usually expects a minor addition like a conservatory to match into the surrounding buildings in a conservation area. (Bartholomew Conservatories)

FIG. 82 Adding a conservatory on to a listed building requires a skilled designer. (Town & Country Masterworks in Glass)

Watchpoint

If a building is listed, even modern, unsympathetic parts of it are protected and need Listed Building consent to be changed.

FIG. 83 Some houses in the countryside are visible from many miles away. The local authority will place strict limitations on what you can build in a National Park. (Amdega Ltd)

Areas of Outstanding Natural Beauty and National Parks

These areas are more about protecting the character of the countryside than the buildings, but permitted development rights are usually restricted. The addition of a conservatory will be assessed for its impact on the landscape and the setting of a house. Often the concern is to preserve a rural, traditional feeling to villages and individual buildings, which conservatories do not necessarily complement.

Tree Preservation Orders

If the council decides that a tree or group of trees is important to the character and amenity of an area, it may place a Tree Preservation Order (TPO) on them. This means that any significant work to the tree, such as pruning, has to be approved by the local authority Tree Preservation Officer in advance and any protected tree cannot be felled without the council's agreement. If a protected tree has to be felled to make room for a conservatory, it may not be possible to build it at all. But if the footprint of the conservatory is too close, a tree can be killed or adversely affected and again, the council's approval would be necessary to allow the tree to be removed.

There are ways of getting around TPOs, such as proving that the tree is diseased or a threat to the foundations of the existing house and offering to plant a new tree as a replacement. But if the tree is healthy and in good condition, it is very likely that it will have to stay. Trees in Conservation Areas enjoy the same protection as those subject to TPOs.

Watchpoint

As a rule of thumb, if you are closer than one and a half times the radius of the normal spread of a tree, it may be adversely affected.

HOW TO MAKE AN APPLICATION FOR PLANNING PERMISSION

Before Design Work has Commenced

If you want to find out whether you will need Planning Permission, or need an indication as to what may or may not be allowed, go and discuss the matter with a Planning Officer for your area. Most councils prefer people to talk to them early about a proposed building project because it reduces the workload once an application has been submitted and makes the whole process run more smoothly. At any time during office hours there is usually a 'duty planner' available at the council offices to deal with day-to-day enquiries from the public, so you don't even have to make an appointment. However, due to recent legislation in the UK some planning departments have stopped providing preliminary advice. If this is the case with your local authority, seek professional advice.

Planning Officers have a high workload and may be reluctant to make a site visit unless and until an Application for Planning Permission has been made. Ideally, take along a scale map of your house and its surrounding area (available either from the local authority, or an Ordnance Survey map supplier). Also take along photographs of your house and the houses next door and, if possible, manufacturer's catalogues to indicate the size and scale of the conservatory. If you are able to specify the approximate size and volume of your house and the new addition this will also save time. Having discussed your proposal, make your own notes of the meeting and ask for a written response from the Planning Officer, rather than relying on memory.

Preparing the Application

It is vital to get the preparation and submission of the application correct, because any error in the drawings or wrong statement on the application could invalidate the permission. For example, if the drawings are inaccurate and the conservatory is closer to the boundary and has an adverse effect on your neighbours, it may have to be rebuilt.

If you use a 'design build' service, the planning application will be dealt with by your supplier, but if you use a DIY kit or supply-only service you will

have to arrange the preparation of the application yourself. Drawings may be obtained from the supplier, a local architect or draughtsman. The drawings have to be done to a metric scale and show plans and elevations of the house, before and after the conservatory has been added.

It is advisable to put the minimum amount of information on the drawings that is necessary to obtain approval. The reason for this is that once approved, you are supposed to ask the council for further approval if you want to change anything. So the less there is on the drawings, the more open your options will be. If something has been left off that the planners want included, they can always ask you to add it after you have made a submission. 1:100 scale drawings should be adequate. Show as little written description of the construction as possible. In uncontroversial cases planning approval is sometimes given without the actual construction (for example, wood or PVCu) being expressly stated. In particular, dimensions and levels should never be given, unless the council insists on them. A 1:100 scale drawing allows some leeway in measuring off dimensions, hence giving some tolerance when setting out on site.

Along with the drawings of the conservatory and your house, there also has to be a site plan of the area around the house, to 1:1,250 scale. To avoid any inaccuracies, most councils insist that it is one prepared by the Ordnance Survey and will not accept a site plan produced by anyone else.

The Planning Application Form

Typically you will need at least five copies of all drawings and the application form, one record copy for yourself and four to be submitted to the council with the application. The form asks a series of questions about the application that are fairly self-explanatory, such as the address, use and nature of the proposal.

There are some alternatives as to what type of application you are making – yours will be a 'Full Application'. The other options, such as 'Outline Application' and 'Approval of Reserved Matters', are used for larger projects where permission is needed before the details are fully designed.

There are some questions about access to the site and car parking (which will usually not apply), whether trees are affected, drainage (which will be to the main drain or a soakaway) and the materials that are to be used for the construction. Along with the application itself are two other standard statements that need to be signed and submitted. One says that you have been the owner for at least three weeks, or that you have notified the current owner. This is to prevent someone making an application on someone else's property without the owner knowing about it. The other statement is to confirm that none of the property is an 'agricultural holding' – highly unlikely to be the case, but the planner likes you to confirm it anyway. A fee must be paid along with the application, typically around £120. There is no VAT to pay.

What Happens Once the Council has Received the Application?

Once the council has received the application, it will be checked for completeness and the date that it has been accepted will be logged. If the form has not been filled in correctly or the drawings are incomplete, you will be contacted and asked to correct them. Until this has been done, the application will not be logged.

If everything is satisfactory, you will be sent a letter telling you the date that the application was accepted and the date you should expect a decision. This is usually in eight weeks' time, and with the vast majority of minor applications this is a reasonable indication of how long it will take. However, do not just assume this and book everything to start on the date you have been given, particularly if there is anything controversial in the application. Allow for the process to overrun by a few weeks just in case.

Once the application has been logged it will be sent to a case officer, who will send out letters to consult interested parties, including the immediate neighbours. If there are no objections or problems, the officers will probably take the decision themselves

using 'delegated powers' and the application may not even be placed before the Planning Committee.

Dealing with Neighbours

If your neighbours object to your application, the planners do not necessarily have to take much notice, particularly if there are no valid planning grounds for the refusal. 'We don't like it' is *not* a valid reason for a refusal. However, if objectors are vociferous, they may force the application to be considered by the Planning Committee and delay the process. As well as this, because these people live next door and play a role in your quality of life, it is in your interests to try to get along with them. Always go to see your neighbours before the application is submitted, regardless of how you think they will receive the news. Show them the plans and try to take account of any objections by amending the plans if possible. The notification they will receive from the council is simply a letter, telling them you are about to build a conservatory, with no drawings or other details. In this situation people often think the worst and may worry unnecessarily, or be offended that you haven't discussed it with them. Even if they still object, at least you will be forewarned of what they are going to say and you may also be able to prevent relations going even further downhill.

Refusal and Appeal

If the application is likely to be refused you may get advance notice from the Planning Officer, particularly if a minor amendment can put it right. However, if the planners decide that it is totally unacceptable they will not wish to waste time with pointless negotiations and so may refuse it as quickly as the process will allow. It pays to check up on the progress of the application at regular intervals.

You may decide to appeal against a refusal if you feel that you have been unfairly dealt with. There is a set period within which you must do this and if the matters of dispute are fairly simple, you may wish to handle it yourself. A government-appointed inspector, who is not based in the area, will make the decision. There is a risk of losing, plus a delay of four to six months before the appeal is heard. So the better option is to revise the design and make another application.

Examples of Typical Application for Planning Permission Forms

Newtown District Council

Development Department
Council Offices
Letsby Avenue
Newtown

APPLICATION FOR PLANNING PERMISSION

Application No ....
Fee paid £...
Receipt No ....

YOU ARE ADVISED TO READ THE ACCOMPANYING NOTES BEFORE COMPLETING THIS FORM.

Four copies of this form completed in BLOCK CAPITALS, the appropriate fee and completed Certificates under Article 7 must be submitted to the above address. Cheques should be crossed and made payable to Newtown Borough Council.

1. NAME AND ADDRESS OF APPLICANT	2. NAME AND ADDRESS OF AGENT (If form completed by agent)
MR AND MRS SMITH 123 THE AVENUE ANYTOWN BORSETSHIRE Post Code **AB1 2CD** Tel. No	JULIAN OWEN ASSOCIATES 6 CUMBERLAND AVENUE BEESTON, NOTTINGHAM Post Code **NG9 4DH** Tel. No **01159229831** (Personal contact name ....**J. OWEN**........)

3. FULL POSTAL ADDRESS OF THE APPLICATION SITE

123 THE AVENUE, ANYTOWN, BORSETSHIRE, AB1 2CD

4. DESCRIPTION OF PROPOSED DEVELOPMENT

SINGLE STOREY REAR CONSERVATORY

5. TYPE OF APPLICATION – PLEASE TICK APPROPRIATE BOX

A ☐ Change of Use
not involving building work

B ☑ New Building Works (Which may also include a change of use) Alterations & Extensions

If box ticked, is application

(i) FULL ☑

(ii) OUTLINE ☐

C ☐ Mining, Engineering or Other Operations

D ☐ Approval of Reserved Matters
Ref. of Outline permission ....
Date granted ....

E ☐ Removal/Variation of a Condition
Ref. of previous relevant permission
....
Date granted ....

F ☐ Renewal of Temporary Permission
Ref. of previous temporary permission
....
Date granted ....

Example of a Typical Building Regulations Application Form

Newtown
District Council

Development Department
Council Offices
Letsby Avenue
Newtown

BUILDING REGULATIONS

Application No ....
Fee paid £..
Receipt No ....

FULL PLANS APPLICATION
Notice of intention to erect, extend, or alter a building,
execute works or install fittings or make a material change
of use of an existing building.
I/We hereby give notice of intention to carry out the work
set out herein in accordance with the accompanying plans.

Signed .... **J. Owen** .... Dated ...... **28/06/04** ......

1. NAME AND ADDRESS OF APPLICANT

   MR AND MRS SMITH
   123 THE AVENUE
   ANYTOWN
   BORSETSHIRE
   Post Code **AB1 2CD** .... Tel. No ....

2. NAME AND ADDRESS OF AGENT
   (If form completed by agent)
   JULIAN OWEN ASSOCIATES
   6 CUMBERLAND AVENUE
   BEESTON, NOTTINGHAM
   Post Code **NG9 4DH** .. Tel. No **01159229831**
   (Personal contact name ..... **J. OWEN** ....)

3. FULL POSTAL ADDRESS OF THE APPLICATION SITE

   123 THE AVENUE, ANYTOWN, BORSETSHIRE, AB1 2CD

4. DESCRIPTION OF PROPOSED DEVELOPMENT

   NEW CONSERVATORY TO REAR OF PRIVATE DWELLING

5. CONDITIONS Do you consent to the plans being passed subject to conditions where appropriate? YES/~~NO~~

6. EXTENSION OF TIME If it is not possible to give a determination within the prescribed period do you consent to an extension of time? YES/~~NO~~

7. Is the building to be put to a Designated Use for the purpose of the Fire Precautions Act? ~~YES~~/NO

8. Do you wish to receive a Completion Certificate on completion of the work? YES/~~NO~~

9. Is a new vehicular crossing over the footway required? ~~YES~~/NO

10. Means of water supply .... **NOT APPLICABLE** ....

11. Details and dates of any additions made to the property since 1948 (this includes garage, conservatory, etc.). .... **NONE**

12. State whether building is private, Council or ex Council .... **PRIVATE**

13. Amount of fee enclosed herewith **£141 INC VAT**

14. Fee payable for inspection of work **£246.75 INC VAT**

15. Estimated total cost of work £ **UNKNOWN**

16. Floor area of proposal Sq. m **35m^2**

This form must be accompanied by two sets of plans and the appropriate fee.
Where Part B (Fire Safety) applies a further two sets of plans are required.

FIG. 86 The Building Regulations require the lower panes of this conservatory to be laminated or toughened to avoid injury in the event of anyone hitting them. (Glass Houses Ltd. Photographer: Hugh Palmer)

Aspects of the Regulations that You Should Know About

Whether, or not, your conservatory requires formal approval under the Building Regulations and is inspected by the local authority, there are certain aspects of its design and construction that should comply with the requirements of the Regulations. Some should be followed because that is what the Regulations state and others because they are simply good building practice. All the regulations are designed to protect you, the occupants of the house and your community, so if you chose not to follow them, you are the one most likely to lose out.

The windows of a conservatory should comply with the minimum heat loss standards of the Regulations, which are expressed by a number called the 'U-value'. This figure results from some complex calculations to assess how quickly heat will escape; the lower it is, the better. The maximum U-value for metal-framed windows is 2.2W/sq mK and for PVCu and timber windows it is 2.0W/sq mK. For comparison, a typical brick wall is about 0.35W/sq mK.

In the unlikely event of a fire in your house, the Building Regulations seek to reduce the risk of it spreading from your house to next door and they do this partly by ensuring that as much as possible of a wall close to a boundary is made of materials that will contain the fire. Because glass is not very good protection against fire, the less that there is in such a wall, the better. The implications for the design of a conservatory is that if a wall is within 1m from a boundary, it should be made entirely of a solid, non-combustible material. Increased privacy and sound insulation are useful side-effects of doing this.

Ordinary glass, with all its uses, is very unpleasant stuff if you happen to bump into it with any force. It can be lethal if walked or fallen into, especially by children, or can cause some nasty injuries if an arm

95

to site without any design work being required, relying on your own skill and diligence to ensure that the design is appropriate. These are normally backed up with comprehensive information on the assembly.

If you decide that you want something more elaborate, once you have expressed a firm interest in a particular company, a sales representative or designer will discuss your project in more detail and make an assessment on site. The company may be a franchise or a local branch of a bigger company, or an independent specialist. Using CAD the retailer may be able to give you a good idea of how the kit will look when finished.

Because of the vast range of different systems and components available and variations in how much work a supplier will do on site for you, it is important to get a detailed quotation. This should cover areas such as the specification of the structure and construction of the frame, the type of glass, the features selected, such as opening windows and ridge vents, and the parts of the building work for which the supplier will be responsible. Most will be able to provide you with further specifications covering the building work required to form the floor and the masonry walls that will form the base on which the conservatory will be built. Some companies will be able to tell you whether a Planning Permission Application is necessary and will be able to provide drawings that are suitable to form the submission if one is needed. If the conservatory is part of other building work such as an extension, you will normally have to get your own designer or architect in to incorporate the conservatory into a single application. If the preparation of a Planning Permission Application is not included, then you will have to arrange this at your own expense. Only once you have all this information, in writing along with a fixed price quotation, can you genuinely compare the cost of one kit with another.

Watchpoint

Some companies make a lot of their money by selling expensive finance packages. Always get a comparison from other sources of loans, such as your bank or building society, before entering into a financial agreement.

When you are negotiating a price it is worth bearing in mind that at 2004 prices, the components for a typical conservatory are worth about £2,000 to £3,000 from the factory, but might be sold for as much as £12,000. The initial cost quoted by many firms is vastly inflated, ready for the salesperson to reduce it dramatically from extortionate to merely expensive, but leaving you with the impression that you have acquired a bargain.

The timescale may also be important. It is not unusual for it to take eight to ten weeks from ordering to delivery and assembly on site by the supplier. Where the conservatory is to be incorporated into other works, you need to be confident that the kit will arrive by the appointed time to avoid delay to the rest of the project.

BESPOKE MANUFACTURER SUPPLIES AND CONSTRUCTS THE CONSERVATORY

If you are looking for a high-quality product, you may choose to approach a company to provide a tailor-made conservatory designed around your individual requirements and the style and disposition of your home. If you live in a relatively well-designed and built house, or your home has a distinct character of its own, such as being a listed building, this route is strongly advised if you can afford it. Anything less could devalue your property. Another reason for this option may be that your house has some particular design problems that cannot be easily solved by using a kit. A bespoke conservatory can cost between 30 to 50 per cent more than its equivalent in kit form, but the end result usually blends better with the house and will probably be of a higher specification. The more upmarket bespoke firms use their own architects and designers as part of their package, because much of their work requires the input of a skilled, specialist designer to make the best use of their product.

As with the kits, you have a number of choices as to how much the suppliers will do on site, but most of them will insist on building the actual conservatory structure themselves. From their point of view, this ensures that the workmanship is up to standard because their teams know the product well. From

FIG. 91 A bespoke conservatory is a quality product. (Glass Houses Ltd. Photographer: Hugh Palmer)

your point of view, you have a single point of contact to deal with if the construction of the conservatory is somehow defective. Bespoke firms are also more ready to organize or carry out the other building work, as well as making submissions for Planning and Building Regulations Approval on your behalf. Many will also advise on, or sell you, other materials, such as the floor tiles or blinds.

To start this process, there is a visit from the company's designer, who will want to spend an hour or so discussing your ideas and looking around the house. There may be a charge for this service. At the end of the first meeting, you are left with some free-hand sketches, a few ideas and a budget cost. If you decide to proceed, the visit will involve a detailed measured survey and a concept design; again, some companies will charge a fee for this stage. Once a

design and cost have been agreed, detailed fabrication drawings are prepared, and, if necessary, Planning and Building Regulations Applications are made. At this stage, you may have to co-ordinate between the conservatory supplier and the general builder (who will build the base and carry out any enabling works). It is important that everyone communicates well from now on to ensure that the conservatory and base dimensions match exactly. The tailor-made conservatory is then assembled in the factory to ensure that everything has been fabricated correctly, and you can usually visit to see it for yourself at this point. Once the base has been built, the suppliers will then assemble the conservatory on site. This stage can typically take anything from one to five weeks, depending on the complexity of the design. From ordering to completion, it could take up to six months, particularly if the building is listed, or there are planning issues to be addressed.

If you ask a company to prepare a design for you, bear in mind that it will own the copyright. The originator of any piece of creative work automatically owns the copyright, unless there is something agreed to suggest otherwise. This means that, having had a design prepared, if you then decide not to proceed with that company, you cannot build it using someone else. If you did so, you would be in breach of copyright and the injured party could, in theory, make you demolish it or pay them compensation. So if you already have some clear ideas as to what you would like and, for example, hand over a sketch plan, make sure that it is absolutely clear, preferably in writing, that you are reserving your right to take the same plan to another designer. If you get into a situa-tion where a design that you want has been produced, but for some reason you do not wish that particular company to supply the conservatory, they may agree to release the copyright for a payment to cover their costs in producing it.

ARCHITECT DESIGN WITH BUILDING CONTRACTOR ERECTING ON SITE

If your planned conservatory is going to have a budget of more than £15,000 to £20,000, it is worth employing an architect directly to conceive a design and prepare the drawings on your behalf. You may well need Planning and Full Plans Building Regulations Applications to be made for this size of project. You will have to pay someone in any case for

FIG. 92 *An architect may design a conservatory as part of a bigger scheme. (Julian Owen Associates Architects)*

this work, but it may be hidden in the overall cost of the conservatory if the supplier does the drawings. If there is any other work to the house to be done, such as an extension, you will almost certainly need more drawings and specifications than the conservatory supplier will be prepared to do for you. The architect may use a standard layout, so that you can go to any kit supplier, or create an individual design that will have to be built from scratch, either by a specialist manufacturer or a skilled general building contractor.

If you choose to employ an architect directly to prepare design drawings, detailed layout plans and specifications, this involves more cost up front, before you actually order the conservatory, but in the long run it should save you money. This is because if you choose a design from a single supplier, it is not easy to compare their cost with that of another company. You can take your own design to a number of different conservatory suppliers, along with a prepared list of what they will have to supply and how much work they will have to do and ask them to quote in competition with others. You will get a keen price based on a standard set of requirements, instead of having to compare a range of different features and prices. If you are not particularly concerned as to the detail, you can even get a general builder to quote against the specifications and leave them to approach their own trusted suppliers to get the best possible price. Usually the builder will add on a percentage for this service, but he may also be able to get some hefty trade discounts, which is a point to remember when negotiating the price.

Any advice that your architect gives you should be entirely independent and objective, so you can discuss the question of whether a conservatory is the right solution in the first place. If the house requires particularly sensitive alterations because it is a listed building or because of its character or location, you will require expertise and a strong design sense to compete the project successfully and keep the Planning Department happy.

For a designer to use the title 'architect', he or she must have completed a seven-year training course and be registered with the Architects Registration Board, a government body that regulates the profession. Many architects are also member of the Royal Institute of British Architects and use the letters

Some of the Jobs that an Architect Can Carry Out
• Survey the existing house and measure it accurately.
• Produce sketch designs and ideas.
• Prepare and submit a planning application.
• Negotiate with planners if the application is controversial.
• Prepare and submit a Building Regulations Application.
• Prepare detailed drawings for a builder to price.
• Identify potential conservatory suppliers and get competitive prices from them.
• Identify potential contractors and obtain prices from them.
• Set up a contract for the building work.
• Monitor the contractor's progress on site.
• Make inspections for quality control.
• Check any requests for payment by the builder.
• Agree any changes to the design.
• Issue certificates approving payment.
• Make an inspection for any defects at the end of the building work.

'RIBA' after their name. The descriptions 'architectural designers', 'architectural consultants' and 'architectural technologists' are not protected in the same way and can be used by people without any qualifications. The suffix BIAT (British Institute of Architectural Technologists) or RICS (Royal Institution of Chartered Surveyors) denotes that they have training and qualifications on the practical side of the construction industry.

DESIGN AND BUILD – THE ONE-STOP SHOP

Your final option is to go straight to a single builder for the whole project, including the design and building of the conservatory. You may chose to do this if you know the builder well, have seen a conservatory he has built, or have had a good recommendation from a trusted source. A reliable, responsible contractor will save you time and help you to avoid a lot of the pitfalls. You will have a single point of contact if anything goes wrong and you should have a better idea of the price from the very early stages of the project.

A disadvantage of taking this route is that the cost is likely to be relatively high, because by selecting your builder so early in the process you will not be getting competitive prices that you can easily compare. In addition, because you have to sign an order before the detail has been properly worked out, there is a risk that you will find that the actual quality and comprehensiveness of the design will not be as you imagined. Should this happen, you will either be disappointed with the end result, or left out of pocket as you have to pay extra for things that you believed were included. Always ensure that you are given a quotation, tied into a detailed specification and at least an outline description of the work – but ideally there should also be a drawing with dimensions and scale showing the shape and overall size of the conservatory.

LOCATING A SUPPLIER FOR YOUR CONSERVATORY

There are numerous companies, local and national, who can supply you with a conservatory. Your first step should be to compile a shortlist of likely companies and there are many ways of obtaining some names to put on it. *Yellow Pages* and, to a lesser extent, *Thompson Directory* are often the first port of call for many people, although the problem with the former is that there are usually so many advertisers that it is difficult to know where to start. Magazines and your local newspapers will also carry adverts, but again it is difficult to tell much about the company. The size of the advert in itself is not necessarily an indication of either the scale of the operation or the quality of the product.

The best way of finding a good company is by the recommendation of a friend, neighbour or family member. Provided it is someone whose judgment you trust, you can be confident that the firm has done good work in the past – although if it was a while ago that the work in question was done, bear in mind that all companies change ownership or staff and there may be a different set-up now. If the recommendation comes from someone you do not know well, or has a link to the company through their trade

or business, tactfully ask if they will receive a commission from the supplier if you place an order with them. This is not uncommon in the building industry, although if an architect or other regulated professional gave a recommendation without declaring an interest, they would be in breach of their code of practice.

Conservatories are a popular choice for featuring in the ubiquitous 'home styling' magazines, which will usually tell you a bit about the project from the client's point of view, as well as the approximate costs. The photography is usually of a high standard and should give you a good idea of the quality and appearance of a particular product. There are some suppliers of conservatories advertising in virtually every magazine of this kind. When deciding where to advertise suppliers will try to match the magazine to the market that they are trying to address, so the type of magazine and how it is presented will give some clues as to whether the firm is right for you. For example, if an advertiser has a presence in one of the magazines that deals with restoration of period homes, it is likely to have design quality as one of its benefits. Such a company is unlikely to advertise in one of the mass circulation women's magazines, where it may get too many enquires from people who do not have the inclination or budget for that kind of product.

Another place where you may find a kit of a reasonable standard is at your local builders' merchant or DIY store. They will not usually provide an installation service, but may provide a home visit to help you to plan your conservatory and provide a technical back-up helpline service. Your local construction industry professionals, such as your builder or architect, may be able to suggest some suppliers that they have had good experience of in the past. Local authority Planners and Building Control Officers may suggest some names off the record, but strictly speaking they are not supposed to do this whilst acting as a representative of their council. As is increasingly the case now, the Internet is another place to find plenty of leads, but it may be better to select from a third-party website, which has a certain amount of screening. Some of them also have a wealth of information and guidance to offer, as well as a list of firms that operate in each area.

Reducing Your Shortlist

After all your research, you will hopefully have a list of possible suppliers that you would like to investigate in more detail. You can easily send for a brochure and may even have a brief conversation over the telephone with them. Once you have narrowed down the selection, rather than just ask for a meeting and a price to gauge how suitable the companies are, there are plenty of other ways to learn more about them.

First of all, what is the immediate impression that you received? In fairness, if it is a small company, it may not be able to produce a high-quality brochure, but are the staff professional in the way that they handle your initial enquiry? Check the literature and establish where the offices are. If all you can find is a mobile phone number, there is good reason to suspect that there is no office and you may be dealing with a very small company indeed. If you cannot get a registered postal address, cross them off your list. It is vital that you are dealing with a genuine business, which you can contact if you are unhappy with the finished result. On no account agree to deal with a firm offering a discount for cash in hand. If they will dodge the taxman, they are capable of exploiting you as well, and you will have great difficulty in getting any redress should anything go wrong if there is no written contract. If possible, visit the office or showroom and have a short chat to whoever is there. If there are examples of the various models built on site, this is a very good opportunity to see whether you like the company's product. You can also ask for some references and the opportunity to see some completed projects, as well as the chance to talk to previous customers.

When you meet the salesperson, think carefully about how they present themselves and their company. If there is an attempt to pressure you to make a quick decision, or unusual discounts are offered, think twice. Do they explain things well, without changing the subject if you ask an awkward question? They should be able to answer all your queries, even if it means checking something and phoning you back after the meeting. You should be supplied with comprehensive information and the opportunity to consider any quotation that they put forward at your own pace. Have they covered all the options available and described what is not included,

> ### Watchpoint
>
> Always follow up references, however much of a tedious business it may seem. If you can't get in contact with someone, ask for another person to contact instead.

as well as all the features of their service to customers? Can they offer computed-aided design or some sketches to help you to visualize what the finished structure will look like?

All suppliers should offer some kind of guarantee or warranty, over and above your usual legal entitlement as a consumer, but don't be afraid to ask for the details. For example, what is covered by the warranty and how long does it last? Just as important is who is backing it. If it is backed by the company itself, a ten-year guarantee may not mean much if it ceases trading the next year. The best type of guarantee is backed by an independent insurance company.

Beyond your own subjective assessment of the company, there are also some independent indicators of a quality service and product. Membership of the Glass and Glazing Federation is a useful indicator. This organization covers all kinds of companies involved in the glazing business, including companies that supply and fit replacement windows, as well as conservatory suppliers. There is a separate group within the structure of the Federation, called the Conservatory Association, specifically for companies which specialize in this market sector. The Association vets potential members by asking for references and checking their books, as well as visiting their business premises. It has a code of practice that all members are expected to adhere to and has a free conciliation service to help if there are disputes. For those who want to get more guidance on the details of how a professional supplier and installer should go about their business, or want some advice on how to approach a DIY project properly, the Association does an excellent and readable series of booklets called *A Good Practice Guide for Conservatories*. However, it is a trade body and even if one of the firms on your list is a member, you should still make your own checks.

Membership of a register that was set up by the Glass and Glazing Federation in partnership with the

---

Tip

If a company sports a number of logos on its adverts announcing membership of various worthy-sounding bodies, check that they are actually members. It is not unheard of for unscrupulous firms to claim membership of an organization after letting it lapse, or they have been asked to leave.

---

government, called the Fenestration Self-Assessment Scheme, is also an indication of competence. For several years now, in England and Wales, it has been necessary for replacement glazing to dwellings to be either certified by a building control officer or fitted by a FENSA-registered company. If the conservatory is exempt from the Building Regulations, it is not essential that the suppliers are on the register, but if they are it is an indication that they have reached a certain standard of competency.

Another reputable organization to which makers and installers of timber conservatories may belong is the British Woodworking Federation, a trade body with a large membership in the UK.

Some company adverts sport British Standards Institute kitemarks. Do not accept these at face value. Check what they are actually for, since British Standards cover a multitude of different aspects, including the type of materials as well as good practice for installation and so on. The British Board of Agrément (BBA) issues certificates approving particular products and again it is a good sign if a company is using them, but says nothing about the standard of workmanship or the quality of service you will get.

Most of the other organizations, some of which are for building contractors, have various membership criteria. Nonetheless, they are fairly toothless when it comes to sorting out any problems, or preventing bad practice, despite their elaborate logos and grand claims. Indeed, some of them only require an annual subscription for membership.

HOW TO INVITE BUILDING CONTRACTORS TO TENDER PRICES

If your supplier will not help with the foundations and walls, or if you wish to get some competitive prices for their construction, you will need to find some local builders to quote for the work. The methods already stated for finding suppliers still apply.

You are likely to be seeking a reasonably priced local builder, unless your project is specialist or has a particularly big budget. There is no harm in keeping an eye out for small building projects under way in your neighbourhood and noting their names and contact details. The nature of this kind of builder is that they do not necessarily come across as slick salesmen. Since good builders are all too rare and get

---

Checklist

You should look for the following points when seeking a conservatory supplier:

- wide range of designs from which to choose
- bona fide business address
- professional way of dealing with initial enquiries
- straight dealing with financial matters
- no pressure to buy quickly, or strange deals offered
- straight answers to questions
- mention of disadvantages as well as advantages of a design
- comprehensive description of the options available

- clear explanation of what is not included in the service
- offer of a written contract that is detailed but not incomprehensible
- five- to ten-year third-party warranty for all aspects of the work, including the appearance
- reasonably good delivery time
- FENSA registration
- membership of the Glass and Glazing Federation/Conservatory Association
- BSI kitemark for relevant aspects of the products
- BBA certificate for the products that are installed.

---

much of their work by personal recommendation, the best of the breed do not have to go to any great lengths to market themselves. They may not even have a signboard up, which is just about the most basic form of self-promotion that you can get. You could talk to the men on site directly, but it is essential to talk to the householder as well, preferably when the project is over, but definitely when the workmen have left for the day. You should also try to meet the 'gaffer' in person, rather than deal with the matter over the telephone. Even for relatively minor building projects, you are likely to have the firm literally on your doorstep for several weeks and having the right people there will be important for you and your family.

Most local authorities require many thousands of small items of general maintenance to be carried out on their properties over the year and will use some small local firms to do some of it. Being bureaucrats, councils have an exacting system of vetting all companies that they deal with, and they usually make the list available to the public. If a firm is on a local authority approved contractor list, you can be reasonably sure that you are dealing with a reliable, decent company (although that can never be guaranteed). However, these qualifications will come at a price and you may have to wait for them to become available once you have given them the contract.

Another way that builders may attract your attention is by mailshot. As with other suppliers, be wary of the handbill that gives no address or contact details other than a mobile phone number. If you call them on the latter, ask for a land line and ring them back on it, to establish it is genuine. Once you get an address, also check its bona fides.

Ideally, you should have at least three prices in order to judge whether the lowest tender is a good deal. This means that you should ask for tenders from at least four builders, to allow for the inevitable 'drop out'. Small builders live a precarious life, which involves tendering for many projects and hoping that they don't get them all because then they would have too much work, but they need to get at least some to stay in business. So although an offer to tender a price may be gratefully received early on, they may back out from submitting a price at the last minute if one their other tenders is unexpectedly successful.

Checklist

You can find building contractors in the following ways:

- personal recommendation
- *Yellow Pages*
- adverts in the local papers
- builders' merchants
- local authority approved lists
- Internet sites
- signboards outside small building projects in your area
- contractors who contact you after a planning application has been made.

A fundamental rule of inviting quotations from builders is to do everything you can to ensure that they are all preparing their prices based on the same information. An estimate, or approximate price is unreliable, since it can easily increase once the builder is engaged. A quotation, or fixed price that you can hold a builder to is what is needed. The starting point is to give them a reasonably detailed description of the work involved and a drawing which is to scale and has all the important dimensions clearly marked. You may get this in a form tailored to your exact requirements from your architect, or the conservatory supplier may give you a list of some standard requirements. Remember that as well as the practical requirements dictated by the conservatory design and construction, you will have to describe everything that you need the builders to do, including things like your preferred brick type, where the wall sockets are to go and the colour of the paint to the walls. If you leave these things for the contractor to decide you may set yourself up to get the worst deal available. A conscientious contractor will not want to take advantage of you, so will either ask you to confirm your requirements or make some reasonable assumptions as to what you are likely to need – even if you have not mentioned them when asking for a price. However, another contractor might spot the missing items but leave them out, to keep the apparent price low. When the contract has been signed and the builders are on site they will start to ask for extras. There are plenty of instances where the final price paid to the lowest tenderer at the end of the work is as high, if not higher, than the other tenders. To a certain extent, if you create the conditions where this is the only way to get the job, you shouldn't blame the builder for doing it. Whatever prices you are offered, always budget for at least 5 per cent over it for contingencies, that is for unexpected items that are only apparent later on, or your changes of mind during the building work.

HOW TO COMPARE PRICES

Once you have received some quotations, all based on the same information, you will have to select the contractor you are going to work with. If you have any major doubts about a builder, you should not invite them to tender at all, because that may waste their time, or pose you with a dilemma if they turn out to be the cheapest. If one is a lot lower than the others, then they are the logical choice, but make sure

that you check exactly what they are offering and how they plan to do the work before you place your order.

You must know when the contractor can start and, crucially, how long it will take them to carry out the work. The answer may make quite a big difference, for example if you want to be 'in before Christmas', or there is a baby due. If you haven't done so already, you should take up references and ask the builder's previous clients some searching questions.

Hopefully, talking to previous clients will increase your confidence in the builder you are considering. To make sure that you definitely have the right company and the right price, you should also ask for some details about how they intend to manage the work.

Not all small builders will offer a guarantee as such, but they should pass on, in your name, any that are available from suppliers, particularly if they are buying the conservatory for you. It is an accepted practice in the construction industry for a small percentage of the contract value to be withheld for the first three to six months after a job has been completed; the balance is paid after the contractor

---

Checklist

The following are some questions to ask about a builder's previous work:

- Did the builder start and finish when they said they would?
- Did they keep the site clean and tidy?
- Were they only available at odd times (a sign of 'moonlighting').
- Did they finish the work to a satisfactory standard?
- How did they deal with any minor complaints raised by the homeowner?
- How did the final cost compare to the original tender and were any extras reasonably charged?
- Did the homeowners' children learn some colourful new words from being around the workforce?
- Are the homeowners friends, relatives or business colleagues of the builder?

Tip

Do not pay a building contractor in advance for his work, unless it involves acquiring a relatively expensive conservatory, which will need a deposit when it is ordered.

Checklist

The following are some questions to ask a builder before confirming that they have the job:

- What is their policy on aftercare and what kind of guarantees do they offer?
- Is the necessary insurance included in the price?
- Will they take responsibility for all the making good necessary?
- Have they included fees for any local authority consents that are needed?
- How much of the work will be subcontracted?
- Is the electrical work included, using a qualified electrician and with a certificate at the end?
- Is the plumbing included, using a CORGI-registered plumber if it involves work to the central heating boiler?
- How does the builder expect to be paid?
- Do they have their own written contract, or will they accept one of the industry standard contracts designed for consumers?

has made good any defects that have become apparent during this period. This is very helpful in persuading a builder to come back and put right some of the niggling details, such as plaster cracking, when they are busy on the next project. It is essential, if you wish to take advantage of such a condition, that a clause stating so is written into the terms and conditions of the contract.

If you have several other contractors doing different jobs for you on site at the same time as your general builder (for example, conservatory installers, plumbers, alarm installers, and so on), it is not unusual for disagreements to arise between even the most sweet-tempered of them. These arguments often centre on who is responsible for any mess and who should clear it up. So it is a good idea to nominate the general building contractor to play this role and allow them to price accordingly.

Check who is responsible for assessing whether local authority consents are needed and whether they are included in the price – often the builder will have allowed for neither. Your conservatory supplier may have assumed that the builder will do the necessary investigation and vice versa, but ultimately it is your responsibility to make sure that these have been carried out. Ask about what work will be subcontracted and how qualified the different trades will be for the work.

Make sure that you know what the payment terms are and that you understand them. There should always be some form of written contract, but if the terms and conditions are written in very small print or are written in an obscure way, read them carefully. Get the builder to explain each clause, or get help if you are not clear what they mean before you sign anything.

CHAPTER 6

Materials and Construction

THE FRAME

One decision that must be made before the final design is chosen is which material you would like to use for the main structural frame of the conservatory. There is a limited choice – masonry, PVCu, aluminium, steel, softwood or hardwood. Which you select will depend on your budget as much as which you find most aesthetically pleasing or the best match for your house. If you chose your supplier before you decide on the material you will be constrained by the options that they offer.

Masonry

If you want to use brick or stone for the main structure, then the end result is likely to be a building that appears to have been influenced by the orangeries of the nineteenth century. The advantage of introducing panels of masonry is that you improve the thermal mass of the building, that is, it will heat up and cool down more slowly than a normal conservatory, with the structure acting as a heat sink. This may be a useful effect if the site is likely to get a lot of sun, because it will reduce the tendency for overheating in summer. In winter, the room will take longer to warm up but will retain the heat for a longer time, which is fine if you are going to keep it in continuous occupation, but a nuisance if you only want to use the room for short periods at a time.

PVCu

PVCu, otherwise known as uPVC (the terms are interchangeable), is the most popular choice by far for the construction of conservatories, being cheap,

easy to fabricate and low maintenance. It is a favourite choice for DIY enthusiasts, because it is easy to work and doesn't split in the same way as timber. It is usually strengthened with a core of corrosion-protected mild steel or aluminium, since on its own it is not a particularly strong material. Systems without adequate reinforcing will also tend to rattle in the wind. More expensive systems use stainless steel for the reinforcement, to avoid rust. If mild steel is used, there is a risk of rusting, even if it has been galvanized. In all constructions sealants and cappings must be used effectively during construction to keep rain and moisture away from the metal reinforcement. There are advocates for either of the cheaper alternatives, but neither aluminium nor steel is necessarily superior to the other.

Unlike timber, PVCu does not need preservative or to be painted for the first few years of its life. It just needs a wipe down with a wet cloth every now and then to keep it looking good. The range of colours available is limited, usually to white, brown or imitation wood. The latter is surprisingly deceptive at a distance, but cannot be said to look like genuine wood close up. But however good it looks when installed, in time the plastic will be degraded by ultraviolet light from the sun and will eventually discolour. PVCu is prone to move as the temperature changes, which will cause warping and twisting of the capping (capping is the strip that covers the connection between two sheets of glass). In a properly designed and built system, this is not a problem, although with darker coloured frames it more likely to develop. One system has twin cappings, which allows the panes of glass to move independently of each other, thus reducing the effect of the thermal movement.

All the budget framing systems are PVCu, but there is big difference in the cost and quality, so it is difficult to compare one system with another without knowing and comparing the detailed specifications. The biggest factor that determines the strength and cost is the thickness of the frame itself – 60mm to 65mm is typical.

The biggest disadvantage of PVCu is probably its appearance. It will never look traditional and all except the most skilfully designed conservatories tend to appear as a modern addition when built on to older houses. More modern houses, which already have PVCu glazing, will not suffer from a conservatory manufactured from the same material. If a house has timber windows that are not in particularly good condition and the budget allows, it will help the conservatory to blend in better if the windows are replaced with PVCu at the same time.

Aluminium/Steel

All-metal systems are more expensive than PVCu, but are significantly stronger. As mentioned above, many PVCu systems require a metal core to be self-supporting, and any structural ties or straps also have to be metal. Aluminium and steel frames are especially useful where large spans are required, in areas such as swimming pool enclosures or where special shapes are required, such as curving roofs. The finishes are usually factory-applied, the best being powder coating (in which powdered plastic is melted on to metal), or galvanized (in which a chemical change to the surface protects it). These types of finishes are essential on steel frames in any areas near the sea, as corrosion is accelerated by salt in the air. As with PVCu the choice of colours for domestic conservatory frames is very limited, being usually just white or brown. Because metal is a good conductor of heat, the frames must be thermally broken, that is, there must be a break in the frame between the inside

FIG. 93 A PVCu conservatory.

FIG. 94 A timber conservatory. (Rutland County Ltd)

and outside to prevent it from getting too cold in winter, thereby encouraging condensation. Metal is even more prone to expansion and contraction than PVCu and the detailed design of the seals and gaskets has to allow for this movement to avoid the glass cracking as the frame expands and contracts throughout the day in hot weather.

Timber

Timber is thought by many people to be the most attractive material to use for a conservatory in a domestic setting. As a natural, traditional building material, it is well suited to older properties and period houses. It can be designed and constructed to match in with the existing style of a house and even look authentically old. It is also easier to match to the existing doors and windows, by painting everything with the same paint when the conservatory is installed. A timber structure will need periodic maintenance to keep the appearance and structure in good shape, with regular painting or staining every few years, but provided that it has been properly designed, built and is well looked after, a timber conservatory can last indefinitely.

The timber should be thoroughly treated with preservative, ideally pressure treated in the factory, with fungicide and insecticide added, and any timber exposed by saw cuts made on site treated before painting or staining. Either stain or microporous paint should be used. These will allow the timber to breathe, unlike normal gloss paint. The cost of a timber frame is dictated by the thickness of the frame, the quality and origin of the wood and the jointing system. An issue that is sometimes raised concerns the origin of the wood and whether it has been harvested from a sustainable forest-management system. This is particularly relevant regarding hardwoods, some of which are obtained at the expense of natural resources, such as the rainforest.

Using timber that is exposed to the elements for the roof is inadvisable, since it can become damp and over time, which can lead to the breaking down of the seals around the glass. One compromise is to use aluminium or steel for the glazing system, supported on timber beams exposed to the interior of the conservatory.

Softwood

European Pine (or redwood) and European Spruce (or whitewood) grow relatively quickly and reach a smaller size than their American cousins, which means they tend to have more knots and a larger grain. As a rule, the further north a wood is grown, the slower it grows and the finer the texture. In southern Europe the softwood grows faster and is heavier and stronger. The much larger, older trees in North America produce timber that is more fine-grained and virtually knot-free. It is also more durable and far less prone to warping than European softwoods. Douglas Fir, which is a good-quality Pine, and Western Red Cedar from North America, which is durable and resistant to warping but similar in cost to hardwood, are both suitable for conservatories.

Softwood, apart from being generally cheaper than hardwood, is also easier to work. However, it is more prone to rot and has a coarser grain with more knots. It dents easily and is more likely to shrink and expand as it absorbs moisture in the winter and then dries out in the summer. Preservative treatment is essential and it must be well-protected by paint or stain to withstand harsh weather conditions. Any of the more vulnerable parts of the conservatory, such as external sills or elaborate joinery details should not be formed in softwood if possible.

Hardwood

This is the most expensive option for a conservatory structure, but undoubtedly it looks the best and is the most durable. It is the material of choice for those companies that produce the top-of-the-range bespoke designs. Hardwood grows all over the world, but commercial sources are chiefly from either the temperate Northern forests (for example, Oak) or the tropics (for example, Mahogany). Hardwood has few knots and is fine-grained. Good-quality hardwood is so solid that it doesn't need preservative or a coating such as paint. Left untreated, it matures to a natural-looking state. It doesn't warp easily and is perfect for carving any features or details to decorate a structure. Unfortunately, its desirability is one of the principal reasons for the loss of the rainforest, in which various species of hardwood trees grow in abundance. Responsible companies ensure that the timber used in the manufacture of their conservatories is always sourced from sustainable plantations.

TYPES OF GLASS

Glass is clearly the most important component of a conservatory that will influence not only its appearance, but also how comfortable it will be for the people who use it. Consequently, you should choose the best glazing that you can afford. Give it priority over most of the other decisions that you make. Single-glazing, the most basic option, is fairly ineffective at keeping in the heat and the very cold surface that it presents in winter will also set up cold currents of air, and the space may feel draughty, however well the windows fit in their frames. Double-glazing is an obvious improvement, but this also comes in varying levels of quality. A typical double-glazed unit consists of two leaves of 6mm glass with an air gap of 12mm to 16mm sealed in-between them. The air gap provides the insulation. This can be improved upon by increasing the air gap, or filling it with a more insulative gas, such as Argon, or having three layers, all of which will increase the insulation value of the pane. However, the thicker and heavier the glass sandwich, the stronger and thicker the frame also needs to be. This is why many modern windows cannot successfully imitate the appearance of a traditional, single-glazed window that had narrow spars of wood between each pane of glass.

Low-E glass, which has a special metal-based coating applied to the inside face of the inside pane to retain the heat in a room, is now virtually obligatory under the Building Regulations. It will improve on the insulation provided by ordinary glass by about 30 per cent. The very best forms of double-glazing can cost three times as much as the basic type, but even Argon filling, which is 15 per cent more insulative than air, will provide only a fraction of the insulation value of a cavity wall. As well as coatings to keep the heat in, there are also 'anti-sun' coatings that help to keep it out in summer, by reflecting the sun. Another reason for considering this kind of treatment is that apart from raising the temperature inside the conservatory, sunshine can rapidly fade fabrics and even damage paintings and antiques. To maximize the useful time that you can occupy a conservatory throughout the year, both types of coating should be used.

There are also other coatings and treatments that can be added to a double-glazed unit. Self-cleaning glass has a special coating that reacts with ultraviolet light from the sun to destroy dirt like bird droppings, and it also causes water to run evenly down the glass, avoiding a streaked appearance after rain.

In order to comply with the Building Regulations and also as a sensible health and safety precaution, in places where there is a risk of the glass being shattered, such as the roof or the lower walls, safety glass should be used. The choice of safety glass is between toughened and laminated. Toughened, or tempered, glass is stronger than ordinary float glass, but when it is damaged it shatters into small pieces that have few sharp edges, thus reducing injury if anyone has fallen against it. It is the cheaper option and the most commonly used. The more expensive alternative is laminated glass, which is very difficult to break. It is made up of several layers, which hold together even when the glass is struck with some impact. It will bend, but not shatter, and is favoured where there are also security considerations. It is not an advisable choice if there is any chance that it may be necessary to break through it in an emergency, such as a fire. Laminated glass is thicker and heavier than toughened glass, and will consequently place more weight on windows and door hinges.

Another possibility, rarely exploited to its full potential in conservatories, is decorative glass. Its simplest form is patterned or obscured glass, but there are also possibilities for etching patterns or designs quite easily using modern technology. Stained glass is available in a customized format from some suppliers, but can also be obtained in more original designs from local craftsmen.

If you find that the glass is trapping too much heat after you have had the conservatory built, it is not too late to do something about it. Window film is not as subtle as the protection that can be applied to the glass in the factory, but it will help to keep the worst of the sun's glare out. It can also be used to increase privacy during the day.

THE ROOF

There are two choices for the construction of the roof – glass or polycarbonate. Whichever is chosen, it will have to be able to keep the weather out, carry snow loading and resist the suction power of the wind. Glass is usually double- or single-glazed and is significantly more expensive than the plastic alternative. The cost is not only in the glazed units themselves, but also in the extra strength required for the supporting structure due to their heavy weight. If a glazed roof is fitted, it should be made of units designed for the location, with either aluminium or steel reinforcement. Roofs made out of ordinary PVCu frames without reinforcement and bolted together may not last and could eventually leak. A timber structure is also best avoided unless it is on the inside of a properly capped metal frame.

Polycarbonate is a popular option, mainly because of its relative economy. It comes in various thicknesses, typically 10mm, 16mm, 25mm and 35mm, in a single, double or triple skin. The thicker it is, the stronger it is and the better the level of insulation provided. Anything less than 16mm is likely to be disappointing once installed. Being only translucent, it does not allow a clear view of the sky like glass, but it is a better insulator than glass, reducing the risk of condensation and improving thermal comfort.

Polycarbonate can be tinted a variety of different colours to improve solar control. To gauge the effect before you buy, ask for a sample and hold it up to the sky to get an idea of how it may look. As well as tinting, solar strips can be inserted into the air gaps, to reduce heat gain from the sun, but they also reduce the daylight levels quite significantly. There is a risk of overheating in the air gaps, which causes movement and softening of the plastic. Even without inserts, in summer, it is possible to hear a polycarbonate roof creaking as it heats up in the morning and cools at the end of the day. Anyone sensitive to

> **Tip**
>
> Make sure that any gasket and sealants used with plastic sheet roofs are of a compatible kind. If they are not, they can overstress the sheet and crack or degrade it.

FIG. 95 A glass conservatory roof. (Julian Owen Associates Architects)

FIG. 96 (RIGHT) Lanterns can make interesting features on a roof. (Town & Country Masterworks in Glass)

such things will also be aware of the increased noise level caused by rain hitting the roof, which is much louder than with a glass roof.

The pitch of a polycarbonate roof can go as low as five degrees, but this is not desirable because the lower the roof angle, the more risk there is of a freak gust of wind lifting the roof off. A minimum of eight or nine degrees is preferable. When it is being fitted, care should be taken over the sealing of the ends of the sheets with breathable tape. If this part of the operation is not properly carried out, there could be a build-up of dust and algae in the air gaps. Condensation is also a risk, which is why a polycarbonate roof should not be fitted in wet conditions, since it increases the possibility of moisture being trapped.

Other plastics, such as acrylic and PVCu, are occasionally used (where conditions and fire regulations allow), but polycarbonate is the best compromise between strength, cost and impact resistance.

DOORS AND WINDOWS

Doors and windows need to be easy to operate, resist the weather and provide ventilation to the conservatory. The last function is crucial, but should not be dependent on the window being open. There should be slots above each window with an adjustable grille to allow background (or 'trickle') ventilation to occur all year round. The window design sets the tone and style of the conservatory, arguably even more than the shape, and is an opportunity to give the structure some character. Modern glass is stronger than its traditional ancestors and comes in larger sheets. Glazing bars, such as those that used to be essential to hold the small, square panes of glass that were the

only size available, are no longer necessary but make an attractive feature. If the windows are to have a painted finish, this will increase the maintenance, so another alternative is to created the illusion of leaded lights by placing strips of metal either on the surface of the glass or within the air gap. Adding a bevel along the edges of glass panes can also enhance the appearance. Whatever style you chose, try to visualize what the view will look like through them, as well as how they look from the outside. For example, some conservatory owners only realize that a main horizontal transom runs across the glazing at eye level once the conservatory has been built, when they stand in it and try to look out to admire the view.

Long runs of glazed wall will catch the wind in exposed locations and need to be strengthened, usually with a column of steel or a brick pillar, which can also be used to add support to the roof. All the windows should have slots along the bottom to allow

FIG. 97 The doors should be integrated into the design of the room and the external appearance. (Amdega Ltd)

FIG. 98 Snowguards protect the fragile roof from falling lumps of snow. (Julian Owen Associates Architects)

water to drain away so that it does not build up and harm the glazing seals. Internal sills sitting on dwarf brick walls are best made of either MDF or hardwood, or tiled, because of the risk of condensation, moisture and consequent movement that softwood will suffer.

Doors are an obvious weak point in the security of any conservatory and can be made safer with clawlocks, five-lever mortice locks and hinge bolts if the doors open outwards. French doors should have deadlocks or espagnolette bolts, which shoot bolts into the top and bottom of the frame with a single movement of the handle. The more points at which the door is secured to the frame around its edge, the more secure it will be. For example, if there are three hinges or more on a door leaf, this is more secure than just two.

Windows should have secure restrictors so that they can be left partly open to provide ventilation, but cannot be forced fully open by an intruder if you forget to close them overnight or when you leave the house. All glazing in windows and doors, or where an arm could reach in to open them, should be toughened or laminated glass. The beading, strip of timber, or PVCu that secures the glass in place can be designed to be hard for a villain to detach (and thus to force the pane out), or can be located inside rather

than outside, with no soft rubber seal on which to get a purchase. Frames and locks can also be reinforced for optimum security.

STRUCTURAL STABILITY

Apart from the obvious requirement for it to support its own weight, the structure of a conservatory has to satisfy other conditions. It must resist pressure from the wind, not only pushing on its sides, but also the suction effect that often occurs on the roof, through which the wind will tear off the roof covering if it is not securely fixed. The roof must also be able to support the weight of birds and small animals and, to a limited extent, people. In the winter, snow may accumulate – if builds up to several inches this can be quite heavy, which is why many suppliers will fit a guard on a main roof above, to avoid the snow falling on to the conservatory below.

The required strength of the structure will depend partly on how exposed it is, and this in turn will depend on the locality and the circumstances of the immediate surrounding gardens and buildings. The worst case is in coastal areas, on an exposed site such as a cliff top or an escarpment. Before a conservatory is designed, an assessment needs to be carried out of the site and whether any conditions exist that require

121

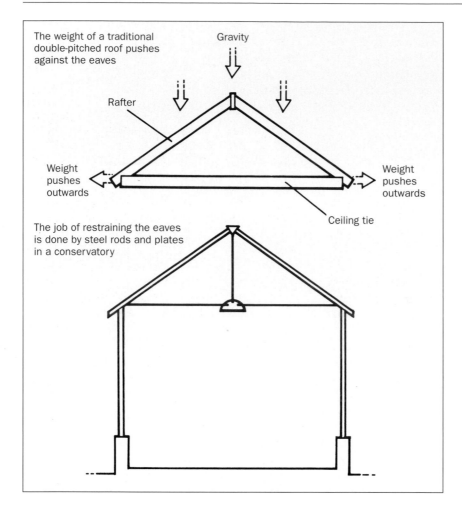

The weight of a traditional double-pitched roof pushes against the eaves

Gravity

Rafter

Weight pushes outwards

Weight pushes outwards

Ceiling tie

The job of restraining the eaves is done by steel rods and plates in a conservatory

FIG. 99 The dead weight of the roof, which tends to push on the eaves at either side, is resisted by steel rods and plates.

more than the usual attention. The easiest way to increase the robustness of the design is to attach it securely to the walls of the existing house, which will usually provide adequate bracing. If the site is very exposed to the wind and weather, it is better to use two or even three walls of the main house.

All pitched roofs have a tendency to spread outwards at their edges, or eaves. With a normal tiled roof, this force is easily resisted by tying the eaves together with the same timber joists that also hold up the ceiling. Since conservatories have by definition an 'open' roof inside, it is not possible to rely on the same structure that stabilizes a normal pitched roof. If the span is fairly short, the stiffness of the walls and the existing masonry wall of the house can be used to avoid the need for ties at ceiling level. But for larger

spans, the roof structure is stabilized by using thin metal rods or wires, usually held together with metal plates. The end result is an elegant structure that can be a design feature.

There are limits on how far an ordinary PVCu or timber conservatory structure can support itself, even with a system of steel ties. Once the roof spans over 6m, some kind of independent steel support is needed

FLOOR

Generally, conservatory floors are constructed out of concrete, which provides a solid, smooth base, ready to take most kinds of floor finish. The choice of floor finish will depend partly on how the room will be used. If there is likely to be frequent foot traffic across it, especially if it is going to be a main route to the garden, a hardwearing finish is essential. Tiles or flag-stones are durable enough for this use and will accentuate the relationship with the outside. They are also easy to clean. If the space is an extension of the living room, carpet tiles or laminate flooring are likely to last longer than ordinary carpet or rugs. Colours should be carefully selected as the dyes used may tend to fade after prolonged exposure to bright sunlight. The fading will be more noticeable when furniture is moved and an area that has been protected from the sun is revealed. If a rug is essential, ideally it should be shifted around regularly to avoid a patchy effect on the floor covering below. Carpet tiles are washable and can be easily moved around. Spare tiles should be obtained along with the initial purchase, so that if at a later date faded tiles need to be replaced you can be sure that they will match. Some laminate floors are not entirely satisfactory in a conservatory, so it is important to make sure that the supplier is aware of the use before a purchase is made.

The conditions experienced in a conservatory are generally not suited to wood block or parquet flooring. The risk of wetting as people walk in from the garden and the extreme temperature range are likely to cause movement and early perishing. Because the conservatory structure itself lacks the thermal mass to absorb the heat build-up in summer, the type of floor can have an effect on how the space reacts to temperature change. A dark, heat-absorbing material such as stone will be cold in the early morning and draw off heat slowly. It will then release the heat during the night. It will also increase the time it takes for the heating system to warm up the space and delay cooling in winter. A non-absorbent material, such as laminate, in a light colour will heat up and cool down more quickly.

> **Tip**
>
> If you want to tie in the conservatory with adjacent rooms such as the kitchen or living room, it would be as well to replace the floor covering in these at the same time. If the flooring is continuous between the two spaces, it will link them visually.

FIG. 100 *The connection between the rods that tie the roof together can be made into a design feature. (Amdega Ltd)*

TRIMMINGS

For many people, how elegant a building looks depends on how well it has been put together. Many people will judge the elegance of a conservatory both on the overall design and the care and attention given to the way it has been constructed. There is a wide range of optional extra design details that can be added on to the basic structure, including casings, corbels, crestings, dentils, entablatures, finials, floor grilles and ridges. On more expensive conservatories these details are hand-carved in hardwood and are almost works of art in themselves. If they are in keeping with the spirit of the overall design, these can be an attractive way to finish the building. However, if there are too many of them on a comparatively small structure, or they are overly elaborate, they can have the reverse effect.

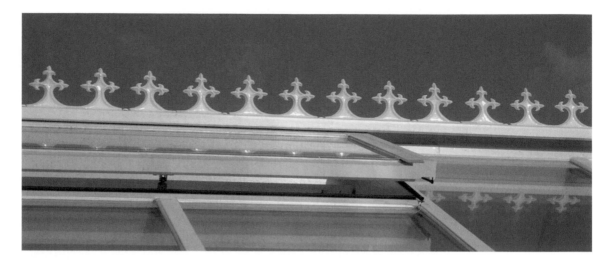

FIG. 101 (ABOVE) The ridge line offers the opportunity to add some decoration. (Amdega Ltd)

FIG. 102 The gutter line and eaves are another chance to turn a necessity into a virtue. (Amdega Ltd)

Even essential parts of the building work, such as the roof drainage, can be celebrated and accentuated, with shaped gutters and decorative hoppers. The latter are available in realistic-looking glass-reinforced plastic, as well as the more expensive cast iron.

The grandest of all the extras that can be added is a roof lantern, which will only look right if the conservatory is large and elegant enough to support it.

COLOUR AND FINISHES

If it is important to tie in the new with the old as much as possible, a timber conservatory will offer more possibilities than PVCu or powder-coated frames. If you want the existing windows to tie in

> **Tip**
>
> If the walls, floor and ceiling of the existing room being joined on to are not already very light colours, change them. This will counteract the loss of daylight after the conservatory is added.

with the conservatory and you have the money, fitting new windows and doors to the openings nearest it will help to do this. Where you are trying to make the conservatory part of an existing room, particularly if there are no doors between them, using the same colour scheme and floor finishes is a good way to achieve an integrated effect. If you keep former external brick walls that have become part of

FIG. 103 The clean, straight lines of classical detailing can be used to create an elegant façade. (Lisa Moth for Vale Garden Houses Ltd)

Items to Consider for Inclusion in a Specification for a Conservatory

Main Structure
- PVCu
- softwood
- hardwood
- steel/aluminium
- purpose-made frames or adapted from standard windows
- Timber from sustainable sources?
- What is the class (grade) of timber used?
- What is the thickness of the structural elements of the frame?

Roof Cappings
- PVCu
- aluminium
- Decorative or plain?

Finishes
- What finish is included in the price and how many coats?
- How much of the finish is factory-applied?
- What range of colours is available?
- powder-coated (aluminium and steel)
- PVCu
- microporous paint
- stained
- natural finish (only certain timbers, e.g. oak).

Glazing
- Triple-, double- or single-glazed
- If double-glazed:
  - overall thickness (e.g. 20mm, 24mm or 28mm)
  - air-filled or other (e,g. Argon)
- Low-E glass
- anti-sun coating
- tinted
- self-cleaning
- safety glass – toughened (tempered) or laminated?
- Which areas will be safety glass – to be for security as well as to comply with Building Regulations?
- Any patterned glass needed for privacy?
- What are the seals used (e.g. Neoprene, Silicone)?

Roof
- Glass or polycarbonate (or occasionally some other plastic)?
- If glass, is it double-glazed, tinted, etc. (see above)?

- If polycarbonate, how thick and how many layers (e.g. 10mm, 16, or 25mm)?
- Is it a purpose-designed roofing system?
- Are there any opening roof vents (there should be), and how are they operated (e.g. automatic, by switch or with a pole)?
- Is the roof reinforced with steel (if needed), and can it take the weight of a person for maintenance?

Windows and Doors
- How many of the windows are opening vents?
- Are there low-level vents and can they be fixed open and still be secure?
- Are there trickle vents?
- Any decorative effects such as leaded lights?
- What are the locking systems?
- Does the door have a five-lever lock with espagnolette bolts (check your house insurance requirements)?
- Can they be fixed in the open position safely (i.e., will not slam in the wind)?
- What is the ironmongery made from and what is its quality?
- Window sills:
  - Are they included?
  - MDF, PVCu, softwood or hardwood?

Rainwater Drainage
- Gutter and downpipe material – PVCu, aluminium, cast iron?
- Shapes and features, e.g., profiled gutters, decorative hoppers.

Trimmings
- Decorative ridges or finials?
- What are any decorative details made of?
- Are they hand-carved or mass-produced?

Builder's Work
- Base construction – concrete slab, concrete planks, suspended timber?
- Exposed brick walls or plastered?
- Any difficult site conditions identified or allowed for?
- Is a stepped lead flashing at the junction of the roof with the house included?
- Is there a cavity tray where the conservatory roof joins the existing wall?
- Is a soakaway and drain run included?

the inside space unfinished, they will make the room feel more 'outside' than 'inside'. Because they are darker than most wall finishes they will make the conservatory seem a little darker than the rest of the house as well, especially at night. If the brick is plastered instead, it will make the room feel more like part of the house, rather than the garden.

TYPICAL SPECIFICATION

At some point before you purchase your conservatory, someone will need to decide on the detailed specification. You should really do this yourself, so that you can compare prices between suppliers, rather than agree a price and then start discussing the detail with your supplier. This will reduce the risk of additional payment being required for extra items of work arising as both parties start to realize that a better specification is preferred to that for which a price has been given. Listed here are some ideas for items to be included in a specification that you should consider and compare between different suppliers. All of them influence the value of the conservatory that you will eventually acquire.

CHAPTER 7

Getting It Built

The success or failure of any building project is usually decided well before construction starts. A successful project is usually the result of thorough preparation rather than luck or experience. Unless you are going to do all the work yourself, you will have to engage and instruct builders, and it is useful to know a little bit about how the conservatory will be built, as well as how to set up a proper contract for the work.

EMPLOYING A BUILDING CONTRACTOR

Assuming that at some point you will have to employ a builder, whether for just the enabling works, or to take on the whole project for you, there is a simple step that will improve your chances of a pain-free project: use a proper written contract. Ideally, this means one that you have arranged, rather than one that the contractor has drawn up. The latter will quite often be heavily biased in favour of the builder. If it is written in tiny grey letters, even if the builder has assured you that the contract is just a formality, read it carefully. The fairest contract to use is one written in plain English by a committee with representation from contractors, architects, surveyors and

> ### Tip
>
> Before building work starts make sure that you inform your insurers, who usually require notification to ensure your cover stays valid. Also remember to upgrade your insurance afterwards, to account for the increased rebuilding costs and extra contents.

lawyers, the Joint Contracts Tribunal, or JCT for short. The Tribunal produces contracts for all kinds of situations and the one that is designed for members of the public who want to engage a local builder is called 'The Building Contract for a Home Owner/Occupier'. It has two versions, one for when there is a consultant such as an architect is inspecting the work and one for when there is not. There are also other standard contracts available, some written by the organizations that represent builders. If you are persuaded to use one of these, or the builder's own version, check that it covers the essential aspects of the work and has reasonable terms and conditions.

THE BASIC ELEMENTS OF A BUILDING CONTRACT

A building project is fraught with potential dangers, especially if you are using a company that you have not worked with before. A sensible contract will anticipate all the obvious problems that may develop and state a way to avoid or reduce them. Most importantly, the act of writing it all down and recording it will reduce the risk of misunderstandings.

The first part of a contract document should state the names of the parties to the contract, that is, usually the owner of the house and the builder. In the case of the builder it may be a registered company, a sole trader or a partnership. If the builder is a registered company or is a sole trader all will be straightforward. However, there could be problems with a partnership and generally the contract should designate one partner to be responsible for the completion of the work. The contract should record the expected start date for the work and a completion date and say what happens if these are not kept to. Some home-owners may wish to include a 'liquidated damages' clause, which will allow them to deduct a reasonable amount of money for each week that the work runs over the date that the work should be finished. This is standard practice in the construction industry and it is reasonable to have a liquidated damages clause in the contract for an addition to a private house. The sum should be modest and be an accurate calculation of your potential loss if the builder takes longer than agreed to finish. However, the right should only be exercised in extreme circumstances, since it is rare for work to begin and be completed on the exact dates that the builder has agreed. This is not necessarily a sign of a poorly organized contractor.

The price should be clearly stated in the contract, as a fixed amount, tied into detailed specifications and drawings of the work to be done. Confusion can result where there is work such as kitchen fitting, alterations to the services, or work to the garden to be carried out at the same time. Ensure that everyone is clear as to their responsibilities and that all the parties involved are talking to each other to arrange the programmes of works. The name of the company who will supply and erect the conservatory should be stated in the contract, plus whether they will be employed by the builder or paid directly by the householder. Many conservatory suppliers will strongly resist being employed and paid by the builder. If you ask for the conservatory to be supplied through the builder, you may find that an extra amount, known as 'attendances' will be added to cover administration and profit. However well planned a project is, there may be some items that cannot be accurately predicted or that may not have been decided at the start of the project, such as diffi-cult ground conditions or the type of floor finish. Approximate amounts can be estimated or rates can be agreed in advance so that if there are extras the homeowner will have an idea of what they may cost.

If the cost of the building is relatively high, the builder will expect to be paid in instalments, a neces-sity for small builders to maintain a healthy cashflow. These can be either at set periods of time, for example every four weeks, or at specific events that occur as the work progresses, for example when the

---

Watchpoint

Never, ever agree to have building work done to your home without a written contract, signed in advance, which covers at least the price and the timing. Ideally, use a standard contract.

Tip

Whatever contract is used, make sure that you have a formal meeting with the builder, with a written record kept. Get the builder to explain the meaning of each key clause and answer all your questions before you sign. Do not sign a contract until you are sure that you understand the implications.

---

work reaches ground level. This method of payment should be stated in the contract. Another construc-tion industry practice that serves clients very well is to hold back a small part of the money due, called a retention sum. Typically this would be 5 per cent on interim payments and 2.5 per cent after completion. The sum is retained for three or six months, after which time any defects that come to light are to be made good by the builder as a precondition to receiving the final payment. The benefit of this arrangement is that you reduce the risk of being out of pocket if there are any defects in the construction work and the builder refuses to rectify them. In fact, any payment that you make should ideally be retro-spective. In other words, the builder gets paid after a section of work has been completed and is not paid in advance. The exception to this rule is if you are asking the builder to pay the conservatory supplier, because there is normally a significant deposit to pay over in advance to place the order for the kit. Ask to see documentary evidence from the conservatory supplier to substantiate the size of the deposit.

It is normal for there to be alterations required to the programme of building work as it progresses on site, either because of something unforeseen, or because the client has a change of mind. It is not always easy to visualize what the building will look like from drawings, or how a space will feel when you stand inside it. Minor changes such as relocating a

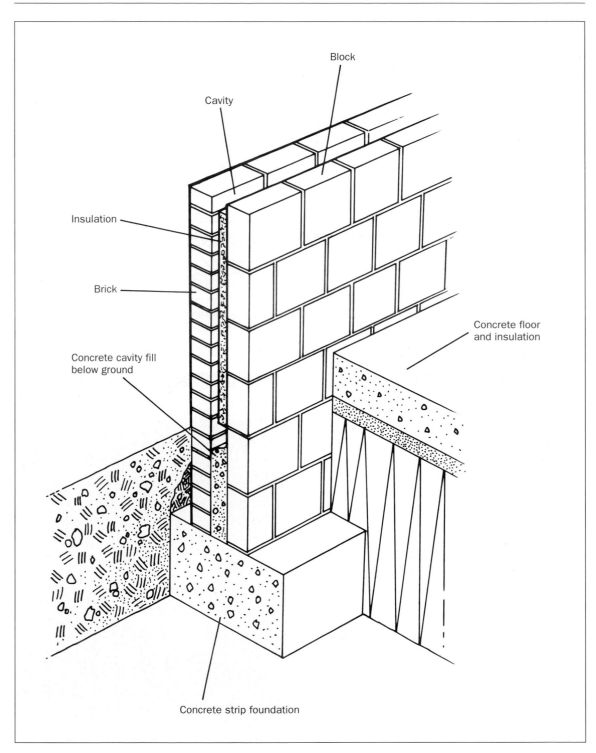

Block

Cavity

Insulation

Brick

Concrete cavity fill
below ground

Concrete floor
and insulation

Concrete strip foundation

FIG. 106 A concrete strip foundation.

Trench fill

This type is most often used where deeper foundations are required, because ground level can be reached quickly and easily. The trenches are usually dug by machine and filled with concrete to just below ground level. They reduce the skill and time required compared to strip foundations.

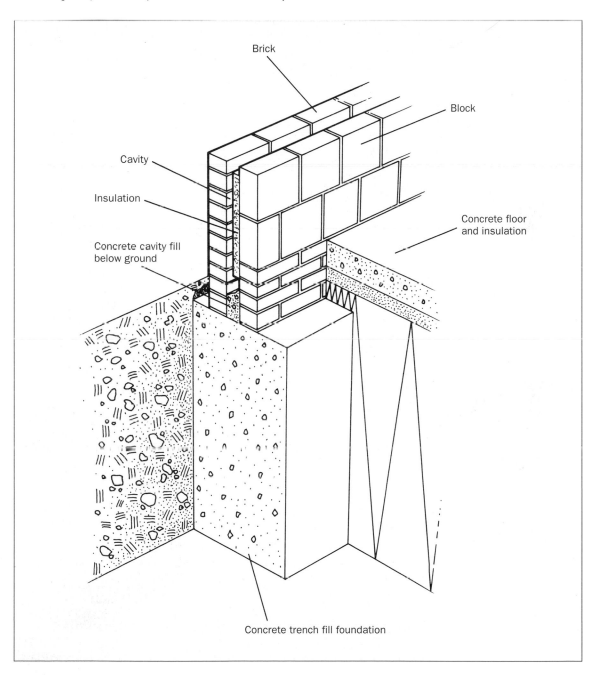

FIG. 107 A concrete trench fill foundation.

Rafts

Rafts of concrete are used for small conservatories. Concrete rafts reinforced with rods or a steel mesh are used where the ground has a very poor, uneven bearing capacity. Rafts allow the weight of the conservatory superstructure to be spread evenly across the ground, instead of just around the perimeter walls.

Pile foundations

Mini piles are sometimes used where there are significant problems with the ground conditions (such as filled ground), as an expensive last resort. Specialist contractors hammer, screw or bore tubes of concrete into the ground, to reach down to better conditions below. Pile foundations start to become economic when depths of 2.5 to 3m below ground are required.

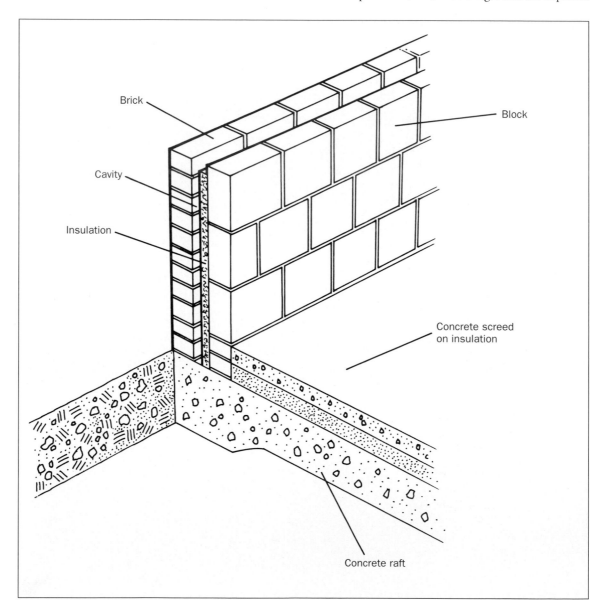

FIG. 108 A concrete raft foundation.

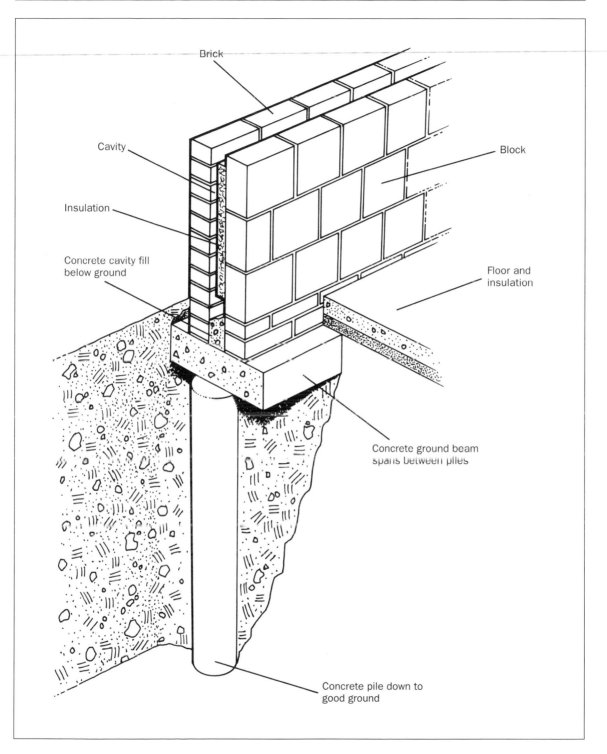

Brick

Cavity

Insulation

Concrete cavity fill
below ground

Block

Floor and
insulation

Concrete ground beam
spans between piles

Concrete pile down to
good ground

FIG. 109 *A pile and beam foundation. This is an expensive operation for a conservatory.*

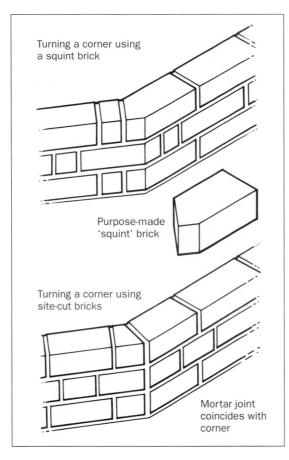

Turning a corner using
a squint brick

Purpose-made
'squint' brick

Turning a corner using
site-cut bricks

Mortar joint
coincides with
corner

FIG. 118 *How to construct a neat obtuse angle in*
brickwork.

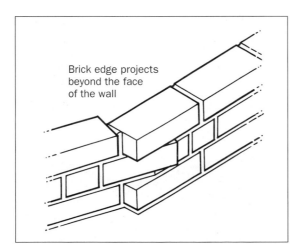

Brick edge projects
beyond the face
of the wall

FIG. 119 *This method is cheaper, but less attractive.*

FIG. 120 *This corner has been formed using cut and*
bonded bricks, but it is almost impossible to tell without
close inspection. (Julian Owen Associates Architects)

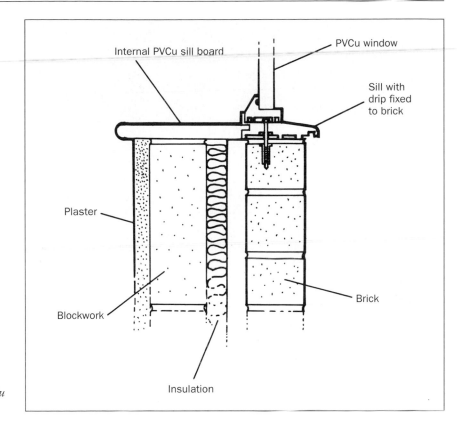

Internal PVCu sill board

PVCu window

Sill with drip fixed to brick

Plaster

Brick

Blockwork

Insulation

FIG. 121 A typical PVCu window sill.

are some good practical reasons for getting it right, which include ensuring that the inside walls are kept dry and that the new addition looks part of the main building.

An early check should be made to ensure that the existing walls of the house are plumb and square to each other in plan. If they are not – and both of these faults are not unusual in older properties – the frame has to be packed out to ensure that there are no gaps that will let in rain and draughts. A certain amount of skill is required to do this neatly, since the gaps are usually uneven and get wider towards one end. If the wall is rendered, it may conceal an uneven or irregular surface beneath. Roughcast render is not an appropriate surface for the inside of the conservatory and will have to be hacked off for this reason, as well as to make a neat surface for the frame to butt up against.

The point where the conservatory roof butts up against an existing cavity wall to the house needs particular attention. The correct way to prevent

damp finding its way through to the inside of the conservatory at this point is to insert an impervious membrane, called a cavity tray, above the junction, to collect any moisture and direct it away from the brick wall. This involves removing some of the bricks and is a relatively time-consuming operation, which is why it is often missed out. If the house was built with a conservatory attached from the start, good practice and the Building Regulations would require a cavity tray as a matter of course.

Sometimes the design and layout of a conservatory dictate that one of its roof pitches is sloping towards the wall of the house rather than butting up to it. One successful solution to this situation utilizes a box gutter that is supplied by conservatory manufacturers. A cavity tray that drains into the gutter should be inserted into the house wall. Sometimes this gutter also supports the roof. A better, but more expensive, method is to use a purpose-made wide gutter that would support the weight of a person and make maintenance easier.

FIG. 122 The junction between the roof and a wall should be protected with lead flashing. (Julian Owen Associates Architects)

FIG. 123 The best way to protect the wall below the junction between the house and conservatory roof is to fit a cavity tray above the junction.

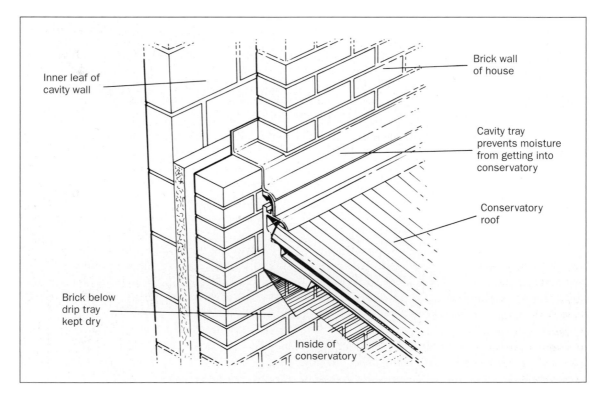

Inner leaf of cavity wall

Brick wall of house

Cavity tray prevents moisture from getting into conservatory

Conservatory roof

Brick below drip tray kept dry

Inside of conservatory

146

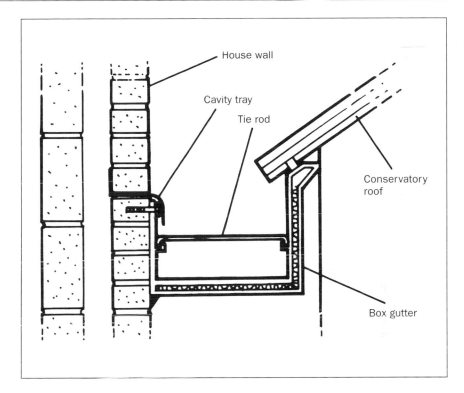

FIG. 124 *Typical box gutter junction between a conservatory roof and a house.*

House wall

Cavity tray

Tie rod

Conservatory roof

Box gutter

FIG. 125 *The gutters to the sides of this conservatory have been designed to allow a person to walk along them for maintenance. (Julian Owen Associates Architects)*

147

them. They can be motorized, to control the blade angle as well as to open and close them. If there are any protruding door or window handles, these can sometimes upset the hanging of this type of blind.

Wooden and aluminium shutters are also available. Although they are cumbersome on a simple conservatory, they make an attractive and practical addition to an orangery or similar space. In a purpose-made conservatory, external sliding and folding louvred or solid shutters could be incorporated in the design.

If none of the above appeals to your personal taste or you want a hand in making your own fabrics, curtains are a perfectly acceptable alternative. They can be of a thin material to let in the light but screen the sun, or more heavy duty to insulate the walls in the winter.

An increasingly popular variant on fitting blinds to the inside of a conservatory is to have the glazing made with the blinds in place in the double-glazing cavity. Because they are sealed in, they do not collect dust and do not need cleaning, but their biggest benefit is that they are far more effective at keeping out heat. They require external controls and to protect the air-tightness of the glazing units, some systems use magnets to move the mechanism between the glass.

Fitting Blinds

Ideally, get the blind supplier to measure up the conservatory, after it has been built. If the blinds need to be ordered before construction is complete, give the blind supplier a set of the plans. Only supply the measurements yourself as a last resort, because if you get them wrong you will have to bear the cost of altering the blinds to the correct sizes. If you do have to do the measuring, use a steel tape rather than a fabric one, and ensure that it is straight and level.

Where the conservatory joins the house, the original wall may not be straight, so it should be checked top and bottom. Fitting the blinds requires care, to avoid damaging the conservatory. If you are going to do the installation yourself, ensure that you have a thorough knowledge of the construction of the frame and have a clear idea where you can drill and fix without causing damage.

FURNITURE

Furnishing the conservatory is a relatively expensive exercise, so consider how long you will need it to last, and whether the chosen pieces will be suitable for the large changes in humidity and temperature that they will have to endure. If the room is to be often open to the elements and will be a main thoroughfare into the garden, the furniture will have to be more robust than if used for elegant dinner parties. Conservatories often create the illusion that they are larger than they actually are, so don't be fooled by this effect into purchasing too much, or items that are too bulky for the space. For this reason you should put off finally ordering any furniture and accessories until you have actually seen the finished structure. Many people find it difficult to imagine what the finished room will be like just from drawings.

If your conservatory is to be an 'outside/inside' room the furnishing should be chosen to reflect this, that is, be the kind of thing that you would expect to find in the garden rather than indoors. If the space is to be used partly to store garden furniture in the winter for use outdoors in the summer, avoid cast-iron frames unless you have a strong back or willing friends to help you lift them – they tend to be very heavy.

Rattan (cane) and wicker (made from young cane plants) are popular choices, partly because they suit

---

Tip

If you want to open your conservatory directly off another room in the house without using separating doors, heavy curtains that can be tied back during the day and drawn across at night will help to reduce the heat loss from your house, as well as making an attractive feature.

Tip

Bamboo and rattan are considered environmentally friendly because they are relatively fast-growing products from third-world countries. Bamboo can grow 400mm in one day, and is used to reclaim blighted agricultural land.

FIG. 140 Garden-style furniture is appropriate for use in a conservatory. (Holloways Conservatory Furniture & Garden Ornament. Photographer: Bob Challenor)

the garden room aesthetic, but also because they will not rot in the damp found in an unheated conservatory in winter. Similarly, any fabrics and other materials should be selected with this in mind, as well as the fading effect of sunlight. For this reason, bright colours are not ideal, because they will show the contrast between faded and unfaded patches. Either light or deliberately mottled fabrics will keep looking fresh much longer, whilst also being in tune with the light, airy feel that most people want to create in a conservatory. Do not put ordinary three-piece suites into a conservatory, unless you can afford to replace them on a much more regular basis than you would have to were they in your living room. Leather is not a good choice either, since it will be hot and sticky when bare skin rests on it in summer.

USING YOUR CONSERVATORY TO GROW PLANTS

Conservatories were originally invented to enable the growing of exotic plants in colder climes, and it is still a reason that many people acquire one. However, some tropical plants need a minimum temperature of 15°C to survive, which is difficult and expensive to maintain in winter. The micro-climate created in a conservatory is more Mediterranean than tropical, so anyone but the most green-fingered would be more realistic to opt for plants that are more tolerant of the cold and will stand temperatures down to about 5°C. For many plants, too hot is as bad as too cold, so steps have to be taken to avoid overheating, including ensuring a good flow of air through the space on hot

days. Similarly, some plants require shade as well as heat and their position has to be carefully planned in relation to the path of the sun. As a rule of thumb, flowering plants prefer the sun more than foliage plants do, and variegated leaves need more light than plain leaves. If the temperature cannot be maintained throughout the winter, annuals such as rapid-growing climbers can be cultivated, which can quickly produce greenery in the summer.

Humidity is nearly as important as temperature, not only for the plants themselves, but also to keep down the most pernicious pest under glass – the red

---

Tip

Plants absorb sound much better than glass, so plenty of plants in a conservatory will make voices and music easier on the ear.

Watchpoint

Never stand the most temperature-sensitive plants near the doors in winter. If a door is left open the cold draughts may injure or kill them.

FIG. 141 (OPPOSITE) *A conservatory is the perfect place to let your passion for plants run wild. (Lisa Moth for Vale Garden Houses Ltd)*

FIG. 142 *Small trees can be grown in this double-height conservatory. (Bartholomew Conservatories)*

Tip

If you want to give the internal landscape in your conservatory some impact, use planting beds, potted plants on window sills, hanging baskets and climbing plants to exploit the full height of the available space.

FIG. 143 *A split level has been exploited to full effect, with plants at several different levels.* (Glass Houses Ltd. Photographer: Hugh Palmer)

spider mite, whose tiny white cobwebs are an unwanted but familiar sight to many gardeners. If the humidity is kept up, the mite population is kept down.

If the conservatory has to be unattended during a summer holiday, the humidity can be helped and the plants watered by one of two methods. The low-tech way is to use capillary action by placing part of some matting in a bowl of water and standing the plant pots on the rest of it. The high-tech way is to use an automatic system that delivers water via tubing. At other times, plants need to be kept well watered, in the form of a thorough soaking once a week rather than a regular trickle because the former will allow them to absorb the water more efficiently.

Apart from the exotic end of the scale, conservatories can be used to extend the growing season for conventional plants. When designing the conservatory, it may be worth considering integrating some raised planting beds into the design. Plants always do better if they have space to spread out their roots, and the chances of them finding the necessary moisture to thrive are increased.

Apart from its permanent residents, in winter the

conservatory can play host to pots that can then be moved outside for the summer. By using similar species inside and outside the glass, the link with the garden can be strengthened. The outside walls of a conservatory tend to be a little warmer than other walls in the house, because of the heat that leaks out, so this is a good place to site more tender plants that have to go outside.

The construction of your new conservatory provides an opportunity to take a look at the layout of the garden, and to redesign it to integrate the internal and external elements. The garden has potentially a lot to contribute to the way that the conservatory functions and is used. Greenery in the right places outside can provide shade across some of

the glass to create a cooler spot indoors, as long as you are careful not to obscure any of the interesting views and vistas that may be available. It can also provide some screening for privacy if there is an open boundary to the garden. The way that people move through the house, under the glass and into the garden should all be considered, and details and materials can be carried through from the garden to help to merge the two spaces together. If the site has some unusual qualities, such as slopes, terraces or water features, these can also be linked into the redesign of the house. With a larger conservatory, focal points normally associated with the garden alone can be brought wholly or partially inside, such as fountains, statues and murals.

FIG. 144 A new conservatory can inspire the redesign of the garden, so that the two areas form a single design. (Glass Houses Ltd. Photographer: Hugh Palmer)